PORT AGENCY

by

Malcolm Latarche F.I.C.S.

WITHERBY & CO LTD
32-36 Aylesbury Street
London EC1R 0ET

iii

First Edition
1998

WITHERBY

PUBLISHERS

© Institute of Chartered Shipbrokers

First Edition 1998
ISBN 1 85609 157 0

All Rights Reserved

Published and Printed by:
Witherby & Co. Ltd
32-36 Aylesbury Street
London EC1R 0ET

Tel: 0171 251 5341
Fax: 0171 251 1296
International Tel: +44 171 251 5341
International Fax: +44 171 251 1296

iv

ICS

INSTITUTE OF CHARTERED SHIPBROKERS

PORT AGENCY

Books in the same series:
Shipping Business Series

Economics of Maritime Transport,
Theory and Practice
Tanker Chartering

British Library Cataloguing in Publication data
Institute of Chartered Shipbrokers
Port Agency
1. Title.
ISBN 1 85609 157 0

FOREWORD

The Institute of Chartered Shipbrokers is charged under its Royal Charter with the dissemination of knowledge, the maintenance of standards, and the provision of a professional qualification. In the dynamic field of international trade and shipping business this is a challenging task.

The Institute has members and students in some 70 countries involved in all aspects of shipping, and its professional qualification is recognised worldwide.

The professional needs to have an understanding of the business environment in which he or she operates. It is also essential to have the ability to analyse the commercial implications of their and others actions as well as the capacity to cope with change.

It is in this context that The Institute made the decision to publish a series of shipping business text books. These combine both theory and practice, and intend to serve the practitioners within the mainstream of shipping business as well as students at college and university and those studying for professional examinations.

The authors contributing to the series are all experienced practitioners in their specific area of shipping business. Therefore in the increasingly pressured sphere of international seaborne trade this series of text books on the major disciplines within maritime commerce make a wide range of expertise accessible to those whose business is, or will be, shipping.

CONTENTS

Chapter One

INTRODUCTION

The role of the Port Agent is one of the most misunderstood of all branches of shipbroking. There appears to be none of the prestigious international dealing in offers and counter offers which the "proper" shipbroker is daily occupied with, neither is there any of the glamour attached to sale and purchase, or the mystique of the intricacies of Worldscale so jealously guarded by the tanker brokers. Nevertheless a proper understanding of the role of the Port Agent should lead the uninitiated to a respect and admiration for the depth of knowledge, commitment and stamina required to perform the huge variety of tasks which an experienced and professional agent may be required to accomplish at any time, everyday of his working life.

These tasks will be examined in detail later but let us first consider why there should be a need for such an occupation.

From very early times trade has been carried out using sea transport. The first sea traders were opportunists loading a ship with goods and sailing (or more likely rowing) to nearby ports. There they would sell their goods and buy different products for sale back in their home ports. The more successful merchants would eventually be able to operate more than one ship in which

PORT AGENCY

case they would have to employ trustworthy captains to look after his interests. As his trading markets increased the merchant may well have decided to take into his employment an agent at regular ports of call.

The agent would assist in finding markets for his master's goods and cargoes for purchase or carriage. Additionally they would be called upon to find crew to man the vessels, labour to discharge them and to pay necessary taxes to the port authority. From these agents we can trace the beginnings of both shipbroking and port agency. Gradually such men would change from being employed by one merchant to being independent representatives of any shipowner he could persuade to utilise his services. This was perhaps made more necessary by virtue of the fact that a merchant with only one or few ships may well have lost them all to pirates or accident leaving his agent effectively unemployed and abandoned.

One can imagine that the role of the Port Agent changed little from ancient times until relatively recently when wooden sailing ships began to be replaced by iron and steel mechanically propelled vessels. Communication has also undergone an unprecedented revolution in the last eighty or so years with the written mail being replaced by telegraph, radio, telex, telephones and electronic mail.

The changes in communications might have been expected to reduce or even eliminate the need for a Port Agent. After all if a shipowner from anywhere in the world can be in almost instant contact with port authorities and service companies in a port to make the necessary arrangements for handling his vessel why should he feel the need to appoint a Port Agent? The answer may be complex and depend upon several factors which shall be examined later. However, it is true to say that despite a period of rationalisation throughout the last fifteen or so years which has seen the disappearance of several long established port agencies in the U.K. and elsewhere there does appear to be a trend for new, small companies fighting to find a place for themselves in a highly competitive market. The long established need for reliable and efficient Port Agents is clearly proven by the age of some companies still in existence and practising as port agents. There are still one or two agency companies which have an unbroken history of more than two centuries of service to the shipping industry. A look into the records of several others will reveal an amalgamation of names of both companies and individuals well known in the great days of sail.

In addition to describing and explaining the various duties of the agent it is essential also to investigate the relationships between the Port Agents and the other parties involved in modern sea transport. To a casual observer the only obvious parties concerned with any given voyage are the shipowner, the shipper and the receiver of the goods. A more informed person may also consider the involvement of a ship or cargo broker, a freight forwarder and an insurance company.

The Port Agent will find that aside from any or all of the above he will find himself coming into contact and having to work with a whole host of other individuals and organisations. These will include the ships officers and crew, customs, immigration, port authorities, pilots, towage companies, boatmen and stevedores. Depending on circumstances he may need to arrange repairs, surveys, medical attention, port state control inspectors, animal and plant health inspectors, P & I attendance, etc. This list is by no means exhaustive but serves to illustrate the diversity of individuals and organisations which at one time or another become involved with a vessel or it's cargo during a port call.

In the following chapters we shall take into consideration the duties and relationships that a Port Agent will need to undertake and develop with all the myriad parties he will meet at some time in his career. We shall also try to establish what standards and ethics an agent should feel necessary to work to in providing a service worthy of professional status.

Port Agents are of course found wherever sea transport takes place. It would be an impossible task to make this book so comprehensive as to cover all possible compulsory duties of Port

Agents throughout the world. It is therefore written to cover the standard commercial practices which vary little throughout the world but when mentioning statutory duties and procedures these will be those applying within the U.K. and reference to law, will be to English Law.

Readers should carry out their own investigations in regard to the regulations in their own area but the information contained here should allow them to understand the basics of compulsory governmental regulations.

The parts of this book which deal with duties towards the ship and cargo interests as well as relationships with other parties can be considered as applying internationally. Readers who are using this book to study for Institute of Chartered Shipbrokers examinations may well find areas of conflict between this book and practices within their own companies. It should be noted that in an ideal world all companies and individuals would work within a code of practice and to standards identical to each other. Unfortunately this is not the case and there is a great disparity between levels of service offered by different companies and the ethics and practices adopted. Should you find that such a conflict applies to you it would be wise to remember that examination questions usually look for the "correct" response.

Much of the Agents work and consequently much of this book will deal with how an agent should assist his principal in complying with National and International legal requirements. It is to be remembered that recent years have seen several new regulations and that much more legislation is proposed for the future. Agents should therefore take particular note of new developments and adapt their working practices accordingly.

Such changes should not be seen as an onerous burden to agents, instead they should be seen more as ways in which an agent can prove his adaptability and usefulness to his principals. Thus safeguarding both his own future and that of a profession which has existed for centuries and by virtue of the efforts of agents past and present deserves to exist for centuries yet to come.

A principal faced with sending his vessel to a strange port will need a reliable efficient agent to ensure that his vessel receives a quick despatch, at reasonable cost. In addition he will need to be satisfied that the agent will ensure that all necessary terms of the contract of affreightment are complied with and that the vessel and its crew do not contravene any local or international regulations.

He will need to know that any money paid by him or due to him is properly handled and passed on to the correct parties at the correct time. In the event of any extraordinary occurrences he will want to be satisfied that the agent together with other necessary parties is able to settle matters in the principals best interests legally and commercially. In short he wants an agent who can do at least as well as he would do in his own home port. The sting is usually that he wants it done with maximum efficiency at minimum cost.

An agent who is able to fully satisfy their requirements is likely to succeed in one of the most competitive branches of shipbroking. However, there is one important aspect which must not be overlooked; today's economic climate is such that there is an over capacity of ships in most of the major trades. Which means that rather than the shipowner being allowed to appoint his own agent the charterer is able to force the shipowner to use the services of the charterers chosen agent. This situation is sure to continue until such time as world trade improves to the extent where cargoes exceed available ships. This event may well be brought forward by the combined impact of Port State Control and the international efforts to improve maritime safety and environmental impact contained within the ISM Code (subjects that will be explored in later chapters). Although the ships that are destined for scrapping will be those that are old and inefficient it will nevertheless improve the balance between cargoes and vessels fit for carrying them.

The Agent Principal Relationship - Whose Agent?

Throughout this book we will look in depth at the tasks the agent will be called upon to perform and the reasons why they are necessary. Before we get that far it will be necessary to look first at the agent/principal relationship.

An agent is a person or corporate entity who acts on behalf of another party (the Principal) and has the authority to bind his principal in matters of contract. Two types of agents are recognised in English Law. The special agent is appointed to deal with a particular piece of business or a single event, thus it will be clear that a Port Agent is usually acting as a special agent.

The second type is the general agent who has authority to act for his principal in all matters concerning the whole of, or a particular part of his business, which may be a geographic area or for certain lines of business. It is important that the agent makes it clear to other parties that any dealings are on an agency basis and that the identity of his principal is disclosed.

While Port Agents will most usually be appointed on an individual call basis and are thus special agents, liner agents are usually appointed to represent all the business of the principal for a specific period of time and over a geographic area, rather than just at one port. Liner agents are therefore general agents.

Beware the different use of the term 'General Agent' normally encountered in a liner context. This reflects the position of a Liner Agent whose agreement with his principal requires him to provide services over a wider field or area, often including sub-agencies.

Traditionally the agent was chosen and appointed by the shipowner but this arrangement is by no means the only or even the most common existing today.

Ships may be employed in the carriage of the owners own

6

cargoes, particularly in the oil and fruit markets. However the number of owners who are able to employ their ships continuously in the carriage of their own cargoes is very small. In common with the majority of shipowners they are forced to offer their ships to other cargo owners to ensure their maximum employment.

Whenever a shipowner hires or charters his ships to a third party he inevitably relinquishes some control of its operation. The degree of control which is surrendered depends upon the way in which the contract between the owner and the charterer is made.

Vessels which operate under charter arrangements are kno' 'n as 'tramps'. This is not a derogatory term and tramp vessels are by no means the dirty, ill maintained ships the phrase appears to imply.

The simplest form of a tramping contract is the voyage charter party. Under this arrangement the shipowner agrees to carry the charters cargo from one place to another. Freight is payable either based on the tonnage carried or sometimes on a lumpsum basis.

The shipowner will invariably be responsible for the port charges of the vessel and the agency fees incurred during the voyage. Having said that it is not unusual for the charter party to include terms stating that any charges and taxes levied on the cargo are to be paid by the charterer. This has lead to some disputes, particularly when the basis for port dues has been changed from a vessel related item such as tonnage to the amount of cargo handled.

The cost of loading the cargo into and discharging from the ship may be paid by the shipowner or taken by another party where the cargo is 'free in' or 'free out'. Other charges connected with the cargo such as stowing, securing, trimming, lashing and dunnaging may also be taken by either party depending on the terms contained in the charter party.

PORT AGENCY

Voyage charters vary considerably and even the standardised forms are frequently amended and added to. There are very few forms which in their original state allow any party other than the shipowner to select and appoint his own agent to attend the ship.

The agent then is clearly a servant of the shipowner and he will be answerable only to the shipowner. This is of course the standard agent/principal relationship and will be governed according to usual rules and laws covering such relationships. Generally this will mean that the agent has to agree a level of remuneration with the shipowner in return for which he will carry out the usual duties required of him.

The law relating to agency may vary from country to country but it is generally the rule that an agreed fee may not have to be paid in full unless it has been properly earned.

At the outset of any agency appointment there should be a clear understanding of what work the agent will be required to do on behalf of the shipowner. Once this has been established the owner and the agent must determine what remuneration the agent is to receive.

An Agency Scale or Fee

The level of remuneration may be a mutually agreed sum or the agent may prefer to operate to a scale of fees. Where the agent chooses to apply a scale of fees, this should be confirmed as acceptable by the owner before any work is done by the agent.

The use of scale fees is common in many countries where almost all agents will charge a common fee for the same duties. Many states no longer permit the issue of common agency fee scales, considering them to be anti-competitive. Agency companies would normally be allowed to establish their own unique scales.

There are some governments which take the opposite view and actually encourage a common national scale. In many states this may even be drawn up by a government and be compulsory.

Under such circumstances if competition is allowed between agents then inevitably owners will choose agents whose approach is more professional and who can be relied upon to solve problems if and when they arise.

An agency scale will lay down different sums for various duties and may vary according also to the size and type of the ship or cargo. Ancillary work such as attending sick or joining crew, may be covered as might the arranging of bunkers or repairs.

For the agent to be able to claim his agreed fee in full it will be necessary for him to perform his duties to a point which can be considered as reasonable. Should he fail to do so the owner would be perfectly justified in withholding all or part of the agency fee.

This could happen for example where the agent fails to complete a customs declaration correctly, even though he has been supplied with all relevant information, and the ship is prevented from working or sailing as a result.

In the past some unscrupulous shipowners have used this rule to avoid paying agents even where their duties have been performed properly. As a result the great majority of agents now demand to have their fee paid in advance together with ships disbursement. This of course reverses the previous scenario in that some agents now feel that having pocketed their fee they do not have to work to earn it.

Choice of Agent

When an owner chooses to operate his ship on the tramp market he will soon come across the charterer who demands some say in the choice of the agent.

There are many reasons why this might be so. The charterer may well be a regular shipper of a particular cargo from a particular port. Indeed the charterer, shipper or receiver may own or operate the terminals at the loading or discharging ports. The owner by contrast may seldom carry that type of cargo from that port and may not even call there again. Under such circumstances the charterer may well be in a better position to select the agent than the owner. Should the charterer do no more than offer advice to the owner then this advice should be carefully considered by the shipowner.

More frequently the charterer will do more than advise the owner and will demand that a particular agent is appointed as a condition of the charter party. An agent so appointed is commonly referred to as the charterer's agent although they are not actually in any legal relationship with the charterer. Care must be taken in the use of this term as frequently a so called 'charterer's agent' may be separately only representing the cargo interest and not the vessel, he would then in reality be the agent of the shipper or receiver.

The charterer may have a genuine reason for insisting on a given agent. As an example that agent may be the only one in the port with experience of the trade. Alternatively the charterer may have had problems with shippers or receivers of goods which only that agent had been able to solve or prevent.

Charterers who demand the appointment of their chosen agent usually do so by amending the agency clause of the charter party to read along the lines of, 'The charterer shall nominate and the owner will appoint agents at each port paying them the customary fee.

The words are usually carefully chosen since the nomination and appointment of agents are quite separate in the eyes of the law. Nomination is merely naming the selected agent, appointment involves a contractual relationship and an obligation to pay.

The freight market in recent years has been such that owners are not usually in a position to reject a potential charter over the choice of agent.

Appointment as charterers nominees may create potential

conflicts of interests in some aspects of the work, although most agents are able to discharge their duties properly on behalf of the owners even though nominated by charterers.

Although we have constantly referred to the charterers agent it is possible that the agent may have been nominated by the charterer at the request of the shipper or receiver. Irrespective of this fact the same arguments apply as if the agent had been the choice of the charterer.

The Protecting Agents

Where the charterers agent refuses to protect owners interests the owner may opt to appoint a protecting agent.

The protecting agents role is to shadow the appointed agent to protect the owners interests and to perform tasks which the appointed agent considers outside his responsibilities. Generally a protecting agent will be paid around half of what an appointed agent will charge.

Some owners consider this as money well spent whereas others see it as an additional expense which need not be incurred. A protecting agent may easily cover his fees by ensuring that a N.O.R. (Notice of Readiness) is presented without delay, maybe ensuring the owner receives demurrage or does not pay despatch money. Proper presentation of N.O.R. in strict compliance with the charter party is one of the main failings of charterer's agents.

The protecting agent is often able to disprove given reasons for delays in working vessels, many so called labour disputes have transpired to be nothing more than the failure of the charterer to deliver cargo to the port on time.

Protecting agents are often able to advise owners on ways to save money on port services. Just because a shipowner is obliged under a charter party to appoint a specific agent it does not mean that he is similarly restricted in choosing suppliers of goods and other services. A protecting agent may be able to arrange reduced costs for services such as tugs, boatman, supplies etc. Great savings can also be achieved under charter parties where the owner is to pay for loading or discharging the cargo.

We have seen above how under a voyage charter party the shipowner is the principal of the agent and is entitled to expect a reasonable standard of work in return for the fee paid. There exists a different relationship between the shipowner and the agent when the vessel is operating under a Time or Bareboat charter, as well as under some rarer types of voyage charter.

Time Charters

Under time charters it is customary for the charterer to have the right to nominate and appoint the vessels agent. This is because the time charterer is more fully involved in the operation of the vessel, and will normally be responsible for all the costs arising from the port calls.

When a vessel is time chartered the time charterer will usually be able to sub-charter the vessel, the sub-charterer also has the same rights. The last sub-charterer may be operating the vessel under a voyage charter. If this is so the final sub-charterer will be in the same position as the shipowner as described previously.

Those above him in the chain all the way up to the head owner will still require the services of an agent at most ports of call. This is because the real owner remains responsible for crew matters and repair and maintenance of the ship, such matters are usually referred to as husbandry.

Most time charter parties contain a clause which calls upon the time charterer to provide husbandry services free of charge. The owner will still need to pay for goods or services arranged by the agent but then he will not enter into a contractual relationship with the agent.

Payment for goods is usually made to the agent by the time charterer who then offsets the costs from the hire payments.

There may be times when the owner wishes to send large sums of money to the agent for crew wages. Should he do this without involving the time charterer, the agent will have to account to the owner and may not use the money to pay expenses incurred on behalf of the time charterer.

The shipowner who never experiences problems is a rarity, when troubles occur during a time charter the owner is faced with a difficult problem.

Firstly the agency services required may be outside the scope of those required to be given under the terms of the time charter. Even if they are the owner may not wish to entrust the work to an unknown agent or one who he has little confidence in.

The owner can then decide to pay the charterers agent to attend to the extra work or he may opt to appoint another agent along the lines of the protecting agent described earlier.

Whichever route the owner takes he will have established a legal relationship with the agent and each party will acquire certain rights and responsibilities.

There are times when an owner will fix his ship on a voyage charter with conditions that call upon the charterer to pay all port charges and to appoint and pay agents. In these circumstances the agents principal will be the charterer and not the owner. The agent will then be free of any obligation to the owner under agency law except those duties which are statutorily imposed upon the agent in his capacity as agent for vessel or master.

This type of appointment is quite different and distinct from the situation whereby the owner allows the charterer to withhold freight sufficient to cover port and agency expenses. Under this arrangement the agent is still answerable to the shipowner. An agent who receives payment from any party other than the shipowner must be careful to enquire why this is so, and to ascertain who his principal is.

An agent mistakenly believing that he is appointed by and answerable to the charterer could find himself in deep trouble if he acts against the interests of his real principal, the shipowner.

The Liner Trades

Ships are not always engaged in the tramp market, liner trades are equally important . Whereas the tramp market is mainly concerned with bulk and oil cargoes, the liner market carries the majority of the worlds manufactured goods. Liner cargoes today are mainly carried either in Container or Ro Ro ships. The mixed cargo tween decker does still operate but usually only on short runs in the less developed areas of the globe or where there are large and regular movements of steel, constructional materials or other mixed cargoes unsuitable for containerisation.

An agent attending a liner ship will be required to perform all the tasks of the tramp ship agent and more.

The most essential requirement of liner operators is that their agents must be capable of generating cargo for the service. This is paramount and liner agency appointments are made on this main criteria, with the ability to handle the vessel in port being taken for granted.

The liner agent will be expected to publicise the line by advertising in the shipping press and trade journals. A mere advert is not certain to attract enough cargoes to maintain a lines viability. The liner agent will therefore need to canvass cargoes by other means. This invariably requires the employment of specialised salesmen who will attempt to identify potential users from local industries, existing customers from other lines, and from more distant ports connected by 'feeder' services.

Liner services are fiercely competitive and in many trades there is a substantial over capacity . In order to remain in business liner agents must be able to secure sufficient bookings to make calling at their port economically justifiable.

Having identified potential shippers the liner agent must have experienced booking staff, to assist shippers in moving cargoes to their destination. Shippers on liner services may have little experience in the international movement of goods and will appreciate advice on customs or other requirements. In view of the fact that the line makes regular calls to the ports on its schedule the agent should be fully aware of all official requirements.

Liner agents will need to quote for the cost of shipping the goods and other connected charges, to ascertain who will pay and to ensure collection of the freight.

Booking staff of the liner agent must have a good knowledge of the IMDG code (International Maritime Dangerous Goods Code). This is a classification by the International Maritime Organization of all types of goods which are hazardous either inherently or in combination with other materials. It is vital that proper questions are asked to enable the goods to be identified and assessed. For example a shipper wishing to load 'sporting goods' could be shipping anything from football boots to shotgun cartridges, the first quite harmless the second highly dangerous. It has already been said that most liner cargoes are shipped in containers which makes easy identification of the goods inside almost impossible . Shipment of dangerous goods in the wrong part of the ship or in close proximity to other hazardous cargo has had catastrophic results in many marine accidents. The liner agent must use every endeavour to identify the exact nature of goods to ensure the safety of the ship and its crew.

Once the cargo is booked for shipment the agent will be required to arrange for the goods to be placed or 'stuffed' inside a container. This may involve delivering an empty container to the shippers depot where they will be stuffed. Quite often a shipper will not have sufficient cargo to fill a container and then the liner agent will have to consolidate that cargo with others for the same destination. This consolidation of small shipments is known as groupage. The comments regarding dangerous goods are of paramount importance in groupage as there is a much greater risk of incompatible materials coming into contact with each other.

Equipment control is another field of the liner agents specialised work. After import goods are taken from a full container the empty box must be 'dead headed' i.e. delivered back to a depot, later it may be required to be positioned at an export shipper's premises. Containers which have suffered damage will need to be repaired and all containers have to be cleaned occasionally. Keeping track of the position and status of each container is a demanding task but given the value of the boxes themselves it is one which the agent must do well. Not all liner agents will be expected to take on all responsibilities for equipment control as some owners will do this themselves. However agents will be expected to assist in finding and recovering missing units.

Some liner agents may find themselves entrusted with the job of stowage co-ordinators. This work involves planning the stowage of cargo in the ship so that the cargo for any given port is easily accessible when the vessel arrives there. This is specialist work requiring the experience of a master mariner. Details of all cargo to be carried is collected from each port on the line. The stowage co-ordinator will then calculate space and weight requirements and arrange for the cargo to be distributed through the ship so as to ensure stability of the vessel and segregation of non-compatible cargoes.

Liner agents will issue 'bills of lading' for cargo loaded at their port. Bills of lading are vitally important documents in shipping. Great care must be taken in their preparation and issuance. Their full importance is described in a later chapter and must never be under estimated by any agent. As well as from issuing bills of lading after loading the liner agent will also need to receive them from consignees before allowing the hand over of any goods discharged at their port.

Many liner agents are also involved in the related business of freight forwarding as the two activities often overlap. A freight forwarder is employed by a person wishing to transport goods who does not have the knowledge or inclination to make the arrangements himself.

Some freight forwarding is done as agent for the cargo owner and some may be done by the freight forwarder acting as a principal. The latter case usually involves a freight differential between that charged by a shipping line and the sum charged to the shipper of the goods. This differential is the forwarder's profit and is retained by him.

Should the liner agent acting also as freight forwarder book cargo on a ship for which he is agent he must be careful to identify the rights and responsibilities of all involved. He must also take great pains to ensure that in his dual role he does not do or omit to do something which might result in a liability towards both the cargo owner and the shipowner.

Some agents work exclusively in either the tramp or liner fields, many others are fortunate to be able to offer both types of service. The liner agent usually has a much closer working relationship with his principals because of the regular nature of liner shipping. There does exist a third category of agent much rarer than those already examined. Some shipowners with large volumes of business to a particular area or country may decide to appoint a 'General Agent' to co-ordinate either port or liner agency activities.

General Agents

'General Agents' will usually fulfill all the usual obligations of port agents, but will also have other roles and responsibilities. The other duties entrusted to a 'General Agent' may well include matters such as the selection of sub-agents at ports where the 'General Agent' does not have his own office, claims handling, the placing of insurance, broking, bunker supplies and financial services. All 'General Agents' are general agents in law, but remember that liner agents are also general agents in law even if not so described by their principals.

PORT AGENCY

The attraction of having a 'General Agent' for shipowners, particularly those in less developed and remote areas, is that they can benefit from being able to call upon the expertise and wide range of services offered in major shipping and commercial centres without having the expense of establishing their own operations there.

For the 'General Agent', who will still earn fees for attending ships, there is the additional income from commissions and claims handling fees. 'General Agents' are not usually involved in the technical management of ships although they will be expected to have extensive contacts in ship supply and repair industries.

In the event of major problems some shipowners are quite prepared for their 'General Agent' to take control of dealings with insurers, P&I clubs and cargo interests.

Agents of any description may find that the freely entered into contracts with their owner principals, are not their only legally binding relationships. The fact that shipowners are likely to be based in a foreign country has lead many port authorities and indeed governments to take measures to ensure payment of their debts. These measures invariably involve the agent, who as the sole contact with the foreign owner, finds himself held accountable for his principals actions. This could mean that by accepting an appointment, the agent is binding himself to stand as guarantor for the owners payment of port and other costs. Should the owner default the agent must make good the unpaid amount. Even more dangerous is the increasing tendency that someone must always be responsible for acts resulting in death, injuries, damage to property. and pollution. This obligation of the agent may be enshrined either in statute law or in port regulations.

Chapter Two

THE AGENT AND AUTHORITY

Routine Work

During the course of his duties an agent will be required to deal with many different governmental bodies and with organisations delegated power and authority by government.

A great deal of this work will be routine form filling, and providing information about the vessel, her crew and passengers, and any cargo to be loaded, discharged or in transit. Although the information requested is generally of a mundane nature it does allow national governments to build up an accurate picture of trade patterns and to formulate policies on maritime matters. Customs and Excise duties often account for a large proportion of a nations revenue and without strictly enforced customs regimes many less well developed states would be deprived of much needed resources.

Occasionally, however, contact with authority is the result of some rather more serious act, occurrence or omission and this will inevitably result in extra work and problems for the agent. It is vital that an agent knows what courses of action are open to him in such cases and how far he will be able to assist his principals without jeopardising his own position.

PORT AGENCY

Routine requirements, as already mentioned, consist mainly of completing various forms.

Although each state will have many of its own unique requirements, there are a large number of harmonised regulations issued pursuant to the various conventions on Safety of Life at Sea, Loadlines, Tonnage Measurements etc. Such conventions are generally initiated under the auspices of the International Maritime Organization (IMO). The IMO is an agency of the United Nations based in London concerned with marine safety and environmental protection. In addition most nations today have some form of Port State Control, This can either be unique to an individual state and operated independently, or as appears to be happening more and more jointly agreed and operated by several countries acting together to enforce measures designed to remove sub-standard ships and operators. The EC and most of the major other European countries act in accordance with the Paris memorandum of 1982.

In the rest of the world Australia is among the leaders in enforcing IMO and international rules and the U.S.A. and Canada both demand satisfactory insurance and financial guarantees against possible pollution from vessels entering their territorial waters. Each year sees more and more countries following the lead of these pioneers and without doubt Port State Control will eventually become internationally accepted and implemented.

From 1998 the IMO sponsored International Ship Management Code (ISM Code) will become mandatory in signatory countries and will require the compliance of vessel operators to a written quality code of practice and management both ashore and on board.

Differing political ideals throughout the world will invariably affect the level of governmental involvement in the shipping industry. For example in many countries ports operate as nationalised industries, whereas when market forces are the driving force behind industry, ports are more likely to be owned by companies and individuals than governments. The modern trend of concern for the environment has forced democratic governments to respect the wishes of the people and to take measures to reduce pollution and increase safety in ports and coastal waters.

Customs

The first official body to be met with in any port is generally Customs. Customs officials are responsible for collecting duties on goods and preventing smuggling. In order to perform this task the Customs will need to receive full details of the ships cargo and voyage.

Mention has already been made of the IMO and harmonisation of international regulations. Many of the forms that agents need to complete for Customs are the result of the IMO convention on the Facilitation of International Maritime Traffic (FAL) held in 1965. All states which were signatories to that convention operate basically identical procedures for reporting and clearing ships. Details of the differences and unique requirements can be found in the latest edition of the IMO book titled 'FAL Convention'. Ships masters are normally aware of the requirements for most ports and the agent should of course be fully conversant with procedures in his own ports. When attending to a loading vessel the agent needs to take steps to identify what requirements there will be at the port of destination. By doing this the agent can be sure that the vessel does not put to sea without some vital document which will delay or otherwise jeopardize discharging of the cargo at its final destination.

The procedures and required forms needed to complete Customs requirements in the U.K along with the reasons for each process are described below. Other nations have more or less similar procedures which must be followed. In some countries not all agents will be permitted to report and clear ships, in such cases specially licensed customs agents will need to be employed. The ships agent will still of course have to supply the relevant information to the customs agent.

Inward Report – Form Filling

In order to report the ship the agent will need to ensure that certain forms have been completed and delivered to customs. The forms may be completed by the agent but it will be necessary for the ships master to sign them. In the U.K. the first form is the General declaration and ships stores declaration. It is a double sided, single sheet form known as the C13, this corresponds to FAL forms 1 and 3 as approved by IMO.

This form is also used for the outward entry and is therefore designed in such a way to allow for information pertaining to either report to be included. An agent who is presented with forms previously prepared by the ship's administration should check that they have been completed properly, and that information is included only for inward report or outward entry as the case may be.

Part A of the form, the general declaration, is quite straightforward and records details of the inward voyage and basic cargo details along with some information about the vessel's ownership and nationality. This information allows the customs officials to verify the origin of imported cargo and the declared destination of exports. Such information is used to ensure the application of correct rates of duties and to prevent trade which may be subject to national or international restrictions or sanctions. Ownership of the vessel is needed to identify the party responsible for charges or expenses of the vessel . Nationality needs to be known for statistical reasons and because it can affect the rates for some dues, as well as the rights and privileges extended to the vessel.

GENERAL DECLARATION FORM

Master's Declaration

Complete this form in duplicate. Complete Part A below and Parts B&C overleaf.
Report and clearance procedures are explained in Notice 69.

HM Customs and Excise

Part A General

For Official

(Name of shipping line, agent, etc.)		☐ Arrival	☐ Departure	Rotation nu
1. Name and description of ship		2. Port of *arrival / departure		3. Date & time of *arrival / d
4. Nationality of ship	5. Name of master	6. *Port arrived from / Port of destination		
7. Certificate of registry (Port; date; number)		8. Name and address of ship's agent		
9.	10. Net register tons			
11. Position of the ship in the port (berth or station)				

12. Brief particulars of voyage (previous and subsequent ports of call; underline where remaining cargo will be discharged)

13. Brief description of cargo (see + below)

14. Number of crew (incl. master)	15. Number of passengers	16. Remarks

Attached documents
(indicate number of copies)

17. Cargo manifest	18.	
19.	20. Passenger return	21.
22. Crew declaration	23.	
24.	25. Deck cargo declaration	26. Are light dues payable in respect of this voyage? *Y

+ You should report the following goods: (a) tobacco products, including cigars, cigarettes, hand rolling, pipe and chewing tobacco; (
except perfumed and medical spirits; (c) cargo in bulk or stowed loose; (d) livestock and birds not shown in Part B, including those
remaining on board.

Continued overlea

For official use

A	D			
•	•	Passenger return		
•	•	OPIC		
•	•	Safety and loadline certificates		
	•	Light dues	Inwards	
			Outwards	
		Other / remarks		

* Report accepted   Date stamp
* Entry outwards accepted
* Clearance granted

....
for Collector

* *Delete as necessary*

23

GENERAL DECLARATION FORM

Part B Stores

If stores are held at more than one location on the ship, a separate list containing the particulars required in boxes 28 and 29 must be submitted location. The total quantities must be shown on this form.

27. Number of places where stores are held	28. Goods in shops, kiosks, etc. *(e.g. cameras, watches, radios, mechanical lighters, clocks.)*	Q
and actual locations :-	....	

29. Name of article	Quantity	
Tobacco .... (lbs/grammes)	....	
Cigarettes .... (number)	....	
Cigars .... (number)	....	
Cigarillos .... (number)	....	
Spirits *(including liqueurs)*		
litre bottles .... (number)	....	
standard bottles .... (number)	....	
other size bottles .... (number)	....	
Wine		
litre bottles .... (number)	....	
standard bottles .... (number)	....	
other size bottles .... (number)	....	
containers, casks etc .... (number)	....	

30. Livestock and birds *(including pets)*	
Description .... (number)	....
Description .... (number)	....
Description .... (number)	....

31. Are any firearms carried on board as stores ? "Yes / No

If 'Yes', please state number ....

32. Gaming machines on board *(number and location)*

Part C Declaration

WARNING:- THERE ARE HEAVY PENALTIES FOR MAKING FALSE DECLARATIONS

I declare that the particulars entered on this form and on any accompanying list(s) are true and complete.

Signature ....   Date ....
  (Master)

For official use

(Arrivals only)

*a) All stores checked   } Under seal

*b) The articles ticked have been checked }   No. ....

-- Signature and grade

-- Station

* *Delete as necessary*

C13   Reverse(02/89)

24

The second side of the form, **Part B**, must be completed by the master as it relates to dutiable goods carried as ships stores. Usually on cargo ships this is limited to the masters representation stock and perhaps a small amount of goods provided as crew allowances. On passenger ships however there is obviously far more in the way of alcohol and tobacco carried and as separate declarations are necessary for each separate location of such goods there may well be several different stores declarations for one vessel. The information given in this form varies in importance from country to country depending upon its policy towards customs duties, alcohol and tobacco consumption by visitors and nationals, and in some cases to concerns over safety and alcohol use by ships officers and crews.

Finally the master must sign **Part C** confirming the accuracy of all information entered on both sides of the form.

The C13 needs to have attached copies of the manifest, passenger list and crew declaration before it is complete. In the U.K. the crew declaration is made on form C142 corresponding to IMO FAL 4.

This form is a list of the crew together with any personal declarable goods they may have in their private possession. Each crew member must enter his own information and sign after which the master will counter sign the complete declaration. The C142 also carries a list of prohibited items which may be confiscated by customs if found on board.

Both the C13 and C142 together with all attachments are required to be delivered to customs shortly after the vessels arrival. In the majority of ports delivery must take place in person at the nearest custom house. There has however been a recent trend towards closure of some of the smaller reporting facilities and it is now possible in some places for the report to be made by fax to a regional custom house.

It is usual to make duplicates of all the documents required for the report. One copy will be retained by customs and one copy remaining on board the vessel. It is also a wise precaution for the agent to make a file copy in case of later need.

The amount of dutiable goods declared on both forms is important because it enables customs officers to calculate what quantities and items of duty free goods will be allowed to be purchased during the vessels stay in port. This calculation is based upon the number of crew and passengers on board the vessel, the intended destination on departure and likely voyage time to reach the final destination or an intermediate scheduled port of call.

If the vessels master makes clear to the agent his intention to take on bonded stores the agent will need to ascertain the next voyage details and pass them onto customs or the bonded stores supplier in order to receive customs authority to purchase stores duty free.

On arrival customs officers may board a vessel and place excess quantities of dutiable goods 'under seal'. This process simply involves putting such goods in a secure place and fixing a customs seal to the entrance. Once under seal no goods may be removed or the seal broken without a customs officers presence or approval. In practice this right is not always exercised by customs but the ships master must still be able to account for all goods which have been taken from the amount declared on arrival.

In the event that a vessel's stay in port is extended beyond that envisaged on her arrival the master may request an issue of stores from those placed under seal. Customs will require full details of the delay in departure before deciding whether or not to accede to the masters request.

Outward Entry

This may sound literally incorrect but is in fact the procedure for entering with customs the basic details of the outward voyage.

Here again the form needed to be used is the C13 but details of the voyage and cargo should of course relate to the outward voyage rather than the arrival.

The outward entry was previously used to determine a ships right to duty free stores since it contained all the necessary details required for customs to calculate crew entitlements. In times past when a vessels sailing was likely to be several days after her arrival the Outward Entry would be done at some intermediate point during vessels stay in port. However, with today's rapid turnaround times the Outward entry is normally done at the same time as the inward report or when requesting clearance.

Clearance

The final act involving dealing with customs is the obtaining of clearance. This is the customs permission on behalf of the government allowing the vessel to depart from its jurisdiction. Before granting clearance customs will need to be satisfied that the vessel has paid or made arrangements to pay all officially regulated dues and charges, has a full set of valid ships documents as required by international law and is free of all restraints.

Today there are very few officially regulated dues and charges, the only charges common to all U.K. ports are Trinity House Light dues, This subject will be covered later in this chapter. There are a number of ports which are run by statutory authorities who have the power to detain vessels until their charges are paid. Generally these authorities will advise customs if there are unpaid charges or alternatively the agent will have to produce proof of payment when requesting clearance. Customs cannot detain vessels for non-payment of charges to commercial contractors unless an arrest warrant naming the ship has been issued by the appropriate authorities.

The ships documents required to be produced may vary slightly dependent on the type and size of ship. In general certificates fall into one of three categories, namely registration, safety and miscellaneous.

Registration documents will be the ships register and/or the International Tonnage certificate issued in accordance with the International Tonnage Convention of 1969. This certificate, once issued, is valid as long as the vessels registration remains the same and as long as the vessel is not altered or reconstructed so as to require a new tonnage measurement to be made.

Safety certificates are issued in accordance with the requirements of the Safety of Life at Sea (SOLAS) convention of 1974 . There are three such certificates required to be produced namely the Safety Equipment, Safety Construction and Safety Radio certificates. These certificates will vary slightly depending on the type and size of vessel and whether or not it is licensed to carry passengers.

Miscellaneous certificates will always include the International Load Line certificate which is issued in accordance with the provisions of the International Convention on Load Lines, 1966 and the International Oil Pollution Prevention certificate carried by all tankers over 150GT and all other vessels exceeding 400GT issued under MARPOL 73/78. Occasionally Customs will ask to see other documents but this is more usually left to Port State Control inspectors.

Providing all the above documents are in order the Customs officer will stamp the C13 and return it to the agent. This document is now the vessels official permit to depart from port and must be delivered to the vessel and retained on board until the vessel clears U.K. territorial waters.

The agent will have one final duty to perform with customs if the vessel was loaded in his port, that is to deliver to the customs house a copy of the ships manifest if this was not done earlier.

The various certificates mentioned above will be further discussed in the next section on Port State Control along with other documents that are of little concern to customs.

Immigration

Usually the only contact an agent will have with immigration authorities will be the delivery to them of a crew list on or before arrival. In many instances this may well be done by depositing a crew list with customs officials. In the case of passenger vessels - particularly those with foreign nationals on board immigration officials will also wish to have a copy of the passenger list. Depending on the nationality of the passengers and crew, immigration officials may wish to conduct interviews on board before granting permission to leave the vessel and go ashore.

If a vessel consigned to an agent has crew or passengers belonging to a state from which entry is restricted or subject to special visa requirements it is advisable to deliver crew and passenger details to the immigration officials as soon as possible, this will allow them to identify any person they wish to interview before the vessels arrival and prevent delays in granting entry rights. This is particularly important with cruise vessels where the prevention and solution of any problems concerning passengers will be one of the agents prime responsibilities.

In addition to dealing with national immigration officers at the port an agent may be called upon to arrange visas for calls at future ports of call in different states.

Agents will also have to deal with immigration officials in the case of stowaways, deserters or crew joining and leaving vessels. This will be looked at in more detail in a later chapter.

Navigational Aids

The UK and the Irish Republic are among the few countries in Western Europe who make charges for the provision of navigational aids outside port limits.

The bodies entrusted with the provision of navigational aids are:- Trinity House, Northern Lights and Irish Lights. All vessels engaged on commercial voyages, tugs and fishing vessels are required to pay towards the provision of these aids. This is achieved by charging light dues to all vessels either on a voyage, annual or semi annual basis. The charges are levied on either the nett tonnage of the vessel or in the case of fishing vessels on the registered length.

Until 1994 light dues were paid by the agent on behalf of the owner to Customs and Excise. Since that time Customs relinquished the duty and it has been passed to authorised collectors appointed annually by Trinity House. These authorised collectors must be company members of the Institute of Chartered Shipbrokers. The Institute employs regional controllers to oversee the authorised collectors and to act as a liaison between Trinity House, The Institute and the authorised collectors.

Despite being proud of the respect for its efficiency the policy of the Institute of Chartered Shipbrokers is to continue its opposition to the imposition of light dues. This opposition to light dues stems from the fact that whilst other Western European countries do not levy charges on vessels they will enjoy an unfair advantage in attracting vessels to their ports at the expense of British and Irish ports. This argument of course can apply only to those vessels and services which have options to load and/or discharge at either UK/Irish or Continental ports.

Interestingly the European Commission produced a report in 1995 proposing that other E.U. countries should follow the British and Irish practice and charge vessels for the provision of navigational aids rather than provide them out of the general tax funds of the countries or the E.U.

Within port limits the provision of navigational aids will be determined by port authorities. In some cases individual ports may join with those nearby to provide local lights and buoys. This co-operation may involve ports in adjoining states. On some busy waterways control and monitoring of vessels movements is vital if collisions are to be avoided. The agent will be expected to provide details of the vessels likely movements to the navigation officials so that they can make preliminary plans. Direct contact with the vessel will be made by radio during manouevering.

Navigational assistance is not limited to provision of lights and markers. During winter the presence of ice poses a severe threat to safe navigation in many areas of the world. The only way to keep the seaways open is to use icebreakers. Icebreakers are powerful vessels with specially strengthened and shaped hulls which enables them to break up all but the permanent ice of the polar regions. Ice breakers generally lead convoys of vessels through ice with the owners contributing to their upkeep by way of special dues. The level of dues is generally banded to reflect the escorted vessels own ice class.

Port State Control

The high ideals and laudable intentions of the various international conventions on safety and environmental issues which have been turned into IMO resolutions were intended to be adopted into national legislation and policed by the member states of the IMO with regard to all vessels registered with that state (referred to as 'flag state control').

Whilst many of the member states have taken proper steps to legislate and enforce it is an unfortunate fact that many other states do not take their responsibilities so seriously. Further more shipowners wishing to avoid the costs and restraints involved in complying with the rules need only move to a flag with more lenient regulations. The use of such flags known commonly as 'flags of convenience' is widespread. It is not a new practice and even before the outbreak of World War II a great deal of tonnage was operating under Panamanian and Liberian flags. For almost 40 years after the end of the war concerted efforts were made to penalise flag of convenience vessels by way of increased port charges. These efforts were not successful for two reasons. Firstly the additional port costs were less burdensome than the financial drain that would have been caused by a return to a home register and secondly the increased costs were levied against ships flying flags of named states, ship owners merely switched to one of the newer registers that were springing up to take advantage of the situation.

Today there are several countries considered as flags of convenience, mostly small nations. The income generated from ships registry can be a major contribution to national income. Some of the more traditional maritime states have recognised that the taxation drain of home flag registry needed to be addressed. This has been done by the establishment of so called 'second registers'. Second register ships are expected to comply with the safety measures but are allowed some degree of latitude in taxation levels and in the nationality of officers and crew.

The benefits of flags of convenience are not confined to taxation and operating costs. Some ships are undoubtedly placed under such flags to avoid the effects of sanctions targeted at nations or hostile acts of countries at war. The situation in Eastern Europe following the collapse of communism has led to many shipowners registering their ships under a plethora of flags not to avoid taxation but to conceal them from organised crime.

In an attempt to ensure more uniform acceptance of the regulations many states have taken steps, individually or collectively with other national governments to establish a system of Port State Control. Such controls allow government to restrict access to its ports only to vessels which comply with standards acceptable to that government. The majority of states which do operate Port State Control incorporate all the internationally agreed regulations as well as adding some further local requirements.

Agents should identify what regulations may be unfamiliar to their principals and advise them accordingly taking special care to emphasise what penalties may be incurred for non-compliance.

In the UK Port State Control is enforced by the Marine Safety

Agency.(MSA) a branch of the Department of Environment Transport and the Regions. In other countries Port State Control may be carried out either by a separate agency or by a port official such as the harbour master.

Port State Control inspectors may board any vessel calling at a port within their jurisdiction for the purpose of ascertaining to what extent it does or does not comply with the regulations laid down by local legislation.

Obviously an agent can have little influence on the outcome of an inspection but by informing the owner of any known deficiencies or problems there may be an opportunity to rectify them before an inspection takes place. Even if the deficiency is not fully rectified the very fact that action is clearly being taken may influence an inspector and prevent the detention of a vessel.

One of the most common deficiencies found by Port State Control inspectors is that of expired certificates. Mention has already been made of these certificates required for customs purposes but there are a number of others of interest to the Port State Control inspectors.

The safety certificates required to be produced for customs clearance are, unlike the registration documents issued only for relatively short periods, and are furthermore subject to annual confirmation by the issuing body. The issuing body will usually be the vessels Classification Society but some certificates may also be issued by the government department responsible for maritime affairs of the vessels flag state.

The first of the safety certificates is the Safety Construction certificate which is issued for a period of five years subject to annual inspection and endorsements. This certificate is not concerned with the quality of the construction of the vessel but with the type and number of bulkheads and general layout of the vessel. It also deals with the fixed fire protection systems built into the vessel.

CERTIFIED COPY

Cargo Ship Safety Construction Certificate

Issued under the provisions of the International Convention for the Safety of Life at Sea, 1974, as amended, modified by the Protocol of 1978 relating thereto (hereinafter referred to as 'the Convention') under the auth of the Government of the Republic of Malta

Particulars of Ship

Name of ship	"RUTA"
Distinctive number or letters	9HRP4
Port of registry	VALLETTA
Gross tonnage	1762
Deadweight of ship (metric tons)[1]	-
IMO Number	7342366
Type of Ship:	~~Oil tanker[2] / Chemical tanker[2] / Gas carrier[2] /~~
	Cargo ship other than any of the above[2]
Date on which keel was laid[3]	AUGUST 1973

This is to certify:

1. that the ship has been surveyed in accordance with the requirements of regulation I/10 of the Convention as m by the 1978 Protocol;

2. that the survey showed that the condition of the structure, machinery and equipment as defined in the above re was satisfactory and the ship complied with the relevant requirements of chapters II-1 and II-2 of the Conventi (other than those relating to fire safety systems and appliances and fire control plans);

3. that in implementing regulation I/6(b) the Government has instituted mandatory annual surveys;

4. that an Exemption Certificate ~~has/~~ has not[2] been issued;

5. that a Lloyd's Register of Shipping Document of Compliance in accordance with regulation 54 of chapter II-2 ships carrying dangerous goods ~~has/~~has not[2] been issued.

This certificate is valid until **21ST NOVEMBER 1999**

Issued at **LONDON** on **13TH JULY 1995**

The undersigned declares that Lloyd's Register of Shipping is duly authorised by the said Government to issue this certi

F.W. ADKINS
Lloyd's Register of Shipping
71 Fenchurch Street, London EC3M 4BS

[1] For Oil tankers/Chemical tankers and Gas carriers only.

[2] Delete as appropriate.

[3] Date on which keel was laid or ship was at a similar stage of construction, or where applicable, date on which work for a conver alteration or modification of a major character was commenced.

FORM 1701(11/91)1/2

CARGO SHIP SAFETY CONSTRUCTION CERTIFICATE

MANDATORY ANNUAL SURVEYS

This is to certify that the ship has been surveyed in accordance with regulation I/6(b) of the Convention, as modified by the 1978 Protocol and the relevant recommendations of the Organisation.[4]

1st mandatory annual survey

Date

_____
Place of survey   *Surveyor to Lloyd's Register of Shipping*

2nd mandatory annual survey[5]

Date

_____
Place of survey   *Surveyor to Lloyd's Register of Shipping*

3rd mandatory annual survey[5]

Date

_____
Place of survey   *Surveyor to Lloyd's Register of Shipping*

4th mandatory annual survey

Date

_____
Place of survey   *Surveyor to Lloyd's Register of Shipping*

INTERMEDIATE SURVEY FOR TANKERS OF 10 YEARS OF AGE AND OVER

This is to certify that, at an intermediate survey required by regulation I/10 of the Convention, as modified by the 1978 Protocol, this ship was found to comply with the relevant provisions of the Convention.[4]

Intermediate survey

Date

_____
Place of survey   *Surveyor to Lloyd's Register of Shipping*

---

[4] Reference is made to the Guidelines on surveys required by the 1978 SOLAS Protocol, the International Bulk Chemical Code and the International Gas Carrier Code adopted by the organisation by resolution A.560(14).

[5] An intermediate survey may take the place of a mandatory annual survey.

FORM 1701(11/91)2/2

РОССИЙСКИЙ МОРСКОЙ РЕГИСТР СУДОХОДСТВА
RUSSIAN MARITIME REGISTER OF SHIPPING

2.

СВИДЕТЕЛЬСТВО
О БЕЗОПАСНОСТИ ГРУЗОВОГО СУДНА
ПО РАДИООБОРУДОВАНИЮ
CARGO SHIP SAFETY RADIO CERTIFICATE

Настоящее Свидетельство должно быть дополнено Перечнем радиооборудования (форма R).
This Certificate shall be supplemented by a Record of Equipment of Radio Facilities (Form R).

Выдано на основании положений Международной конвенции по охране человеческой жизни на море 1974 года, с поправ

по уполномочию Правительства _____ Росси
Морским Регистром Судоходства   (название государства)

Issued under the provisions of the International Convention for the Safety of Life at Sea, 1974, as amended under the au

of the Government of _____ by the Russian Maritime Register of Sh
                              (name of the State)

СВЕДЕНИЯ О СУДНЕ/PARTICULARS OF SHIP

Название судна Name of Ship	Регистровый номер или позывной сигнал Distinctive Number or Letters	Порт приписки Port of Registry	Валовая вместимость Gross Tonnage	Морские районы, на плавание в которых судну выдано Свидетельство (правило IV/2) Sea areas in which ship is certified to operate (regulation IV/2)	Номер IM Num

Дата закладки киля или дата, на которую судно находилось в подобной стадии постройки или, где это приме
дата, на которую началось переоборудование или изменение, или модификация существенного хара

"_____" _____

Date on which keel was laid or ship was at a similar stage of construction or, where applicable, date on which work for a conver

an alteration or modification of a major character was commenced "_____" _____

НАСТОЯЩИМ УДОСТОВЕРЯЕТСЯ:
THIS IS TO CERTIFY:

1. Что судно освидетельствовано в соответствии с требованиями правила I/9 Конвенции.
   That the ship has been surveyed in accordance with the requirements of regulation I/9 of the Convention.

2. Что освидетельствованием установлено, что:
   That the survey showed that:

   2.1 судно отвечает требованиям Конвенции в отношении радиоустановок;
       the ship complied with the requirements of the Convention as regards radio installations;

   2.2 действие радиоустановок, используемых в спасательных средствах, отвечает требованиям Конв
       the functioning of the radio installations used in life-saving appliances complied with the requirements of the Cou

3. Что выдано/не выдано* Свидетельство об изъятии   №
   That an Exemption Certificate has/has not* been issued.

Настоящее Свидетельство действительно до _____
This Certificate is valid until

Выдано в _____
Issued at
        (место выдачи Свидетельства)
        place of issue of Certificate

Российский Морской Регистр Судоходства
Russian Maritime Register of Shipping

подпись уполномоченного лица,
выдавшего Свидетельство
signature of authorized official
issuing the Certificate

№ _____

Печать или штамп организации,
выдавшей Свидетельство
Seal or stamp of the issuing authority,
as appropriate

_____
* Ненужное зачеркнуть.
  Delete as appropriate.

CERTIFIED COPY

N°. **BRS 5002!**
Page 1 of 2

Cargo Ship Safety Equipment Certificate

This Certificate shall be supplemented by a Record of Equipment (Form E), N° 7342366/02

Issued under the provisions of the International Convention for the Safety of Life at Sea, 1974, as amended, and modified by the Protocol of 1978 relating thereto (hereinafter referred to as 'the Convention') under the authority of the Government of THE REPUBLIC OF MALTA

Particulars of Ship

Name of ship	RUTA
Distinctive number or letters	9HRP4
Port of registry	VALLETTA
Gross tonnage	1593 *
Deadweight of ship (metric tons)[1]	–
Length of ship (regulation III/3.10)	71.81
IMO Number	7342366
Type of Ship:	~~Oil tanker² / Chemical tanker² / Gas carrier²~~ / Cargo ship other than any of the above²
Date on which keel was laid[3]	08.1973

This is to certify:

1. that the ship has been surveyed in accordance with the requirements of regulation I/8 of the Convention a modified by the 1978 Protocol relating thereto;

2. that the survey showed that:

    2.1 the ship complied with the requirements of the Convention as regards fire safety systems and appliances and fire control plans;

    2.2 the life-saving appliances and the equipment of the lifeboats, liferafts and rescue boats were provide in accordance with the requirements of the Convention;

    2.3 the ship was provided with a line-throwing appliance and radio installations used in life-saving appliances in accordance with the requirements of the Convention;

    2.4 the ship complied with the requirements of the Convention as regards shipborne navigational equipment, nautical publications and means of embarkation for pilots;

    2.5 the ship was provided with lights, shapes, means of making sound signals and distress signals in accordance with the requirements of the Convention and the International Regulations for Preventir Collisions at Sea in force;

    2.6 in all other respects the ship complied with the relevant requirements of the Convention;

[1] For Oil tankers/Chemical tankers and Gas carriers only. [2] Delete as appropriate.
[3] Date on which keel was laid or ship was at a similar stage of construction or, where applicable, date on which work for a conversion or an alteration or modification of a major character was commenced.

FORM 1703 (11/91) 1/2

3.   that the ship operates in accordance with regulation III/26.1.1.1 within the limits of the trade area:

4.   that in implementing regulation I/6(b) the Government has instituted mandatory annual surveys;

5.   that an Exemption Certificate has / has not[2] been issued;

6.   that a Lloyd's Register of Shipping Document of Compliance in accordance with regulation 54 of chapter II-2 for ships carrying dangerous goods has/has not[2] been issued.

This certificate is valid until   10TH OCTOBER 1997

Issued at   **BRISTOL**   on   16TH NOVEMBER 1995

The undersigned declares that Lloyd's Register of Shipping is duly authorised by the said Government to issue this certificate.

*   THE ABOVE GROSS TONNAGE HAS BEEN MEASURED
BY LLOYD'S REGISTER IN ACCORDANCE WITH THE
NATIONAL TONNAGE REGULATIONS WHICH WERE IN
FORCE PRIOR TO THE COMING INTO FORCE OF THE   J.M. DANIEL
INTERNATIONAL CONVENTION OF TONNAGE   Lloyd's Register of Shipping
MEASUREMENTS OF SHIPS, 1969.   ~~71 Fenchurch Street, London EC3M 4BS~~

MANDATORY ANNUAL SURVEY

This is to certify that the ship has been surveyed in accordance with regulation I/6(b) of the Convention, as modified by the 1978 Protocol and the relevant recommendations of the Organisation[4].

Mandatory annual survey[5]   *Date*

Place of survey

          Surveyor to Lloyd's Register of Shipping

INTERMEDIATE SURVEY FOR TANKERS OF 10 YEARS OF AGE AND OVER

This is to certify that, at an intermediate survey required by regulation I/8 of the Convention, as modified by the 1978 Protocol, this ship was found to comply with the relevant provisions of the Convention[4].

Intermediate survey   *Date*

Place of survey

          Surveyor to Lloyd's Register of Shipping

Under the provisions of regulation I/14 of the Convention, as modified by the 1978 Protocol, the validity of this Certificate is extended until

       Date

Place of survey

          Surveyor to Lloyd's Register of Shipping

[2] Delete as appropriate.
[4] Reference is made to the Guidelines on surveys required by the 1978 SOLAS Protocol, the International Bulk Chemical Code and the International Gas Carrier Code adopted by the Organisation by resolution A.560(14).
[5] An intermediate survey may take the place of a mandatory annual survey.

FORM 1703 (11/91) 2/2

CERTIFIED COPY

Record Nº   7342366/02
Page 1 of 2

Record of Equipment for the
Cargo Ship Safety Equipment Certificate (FORM E)

This Record shall be permanently attached to the Cargo Ship Safety Equipment Certificate

Record of Equipment for compliance with the International Convention for the Safety of Life at Sea, 1974, as amended in 1988

1. PARTICULARS OF SHIP

Name of ship	
	RUTA

Distinctive number or letters		IMO number	
	9HRP4		7342366

2. DETAILS OF LIFE-SAVING APPLIANCES

		PORT SIDE	STARBOARD SIDE
2.1	Total number of persons for which life-saving appliances are provided	11	
2.2	Total number of lifeboats	–	–
	2.2.1 Total number of persons accommodated by them	–	–
	2.2.2 Number of self-righting partially enclosed lifeboats (regulation III/43)	–	–
	2.2.3 Number of totally enclosed lifeboats (regulation III/44)	–	–
	2.2.4 Number of lifeboats with a self-contained air support system (regulation III/45)	–	–
	2.2.5 Number of fire-protected lifeboats (regulation III/46)	–	–
	2.2.6 Other lifeboats		
	2.2.6.1 Number	–	–
	2.2.6.2 Type	–	–
	2.2.7 Number of freefall lifeboats		
	2.2.7.1 Totally enclosed (regulation III/44)	–	
	2.2.7.2 Self-contained (regulation III/45)	–	
	2.2.7.3 Fire-protected (regulation III/46)	–	
2.3	Number of motor lifeboats (included in the total lifeboats shown above)	–	
	2.3.1 Number of motor lifeboats fitted with searchlights	–	
2.4	Number of rescue boats	1	
	2.4.1 Number of rescue boats which are included in the total lifeboats shown above	–	
2.5	Liferafts		
	2.5.1 Liferafts for which approved launching appliances are required		
	2.5.1.1 Number of liferafts	–	
	2.5.1.2 Number of persons accommodated by them	–	

FORM 2130 (10/91) 1/2

2.5.2	Liferafts for which approved launching appliances are not required	
	2.5.2.1 Number of liferafts	3
	2.5.2.2 Number of persons accommodated by them	32
2.5.3	Number of liferafts required by regulation III/26.1.4	-
2.6	Number of lifebuoys	8
2.7	Number of lifejackets	11
2.8	Immersion suits	
	2.8.1 Total number of immersion suits	11
	2.8.2 Number of suits complying with the requirements for lifejackets	-
2.9	Number of thermal protective aids[1]	-
2.10	Radio installations used in life-saving appliances	
	2.10.1 Number of radar transponders	2
	2.10.2 Number of two-way VHF radiotelephone apparatus	3

3. SHIPS CONSTRUCTED BEFORE 1 FEBRUARY 1992 WHICH DO NOT FULLY COMPLY WITH THE APPLICABLE REQUIREMENTS OF CHAPTER III OF THE CONVENTION AS AMENDED IN 1988

	ACTUAL PROVISION
Radiotelegraph installation for lifeboat	-
Portable radio apparatus for survival craft	-
Survival craft EPIRB (121.5 MHz and 243.0 MHz)	-
Two-way radiotelephone apparatus	-

This is to certify that, on the date of issue, this Record was correct in all respects.

Issued at   BRISTOL

on   16TH NOVEMBER 1995

J.M.DANIEL
Lloyd's Register of Shipping

The Safety Radio certificate is issued for one year only. This certificate confirms that the communication equipment such as radio, telegraph and telephone required for the vessel to comply with SOLAS regulations is fitted and at the time of first issue of the certificate or subsequent renewal was in working order. The communication equipment of the ship will require emergency power in the case of a failure of the ships generating equipment. Emergency power is provided by batteries. The life span of the batteries is also recorded on the certificate and may be checked by Port State Control officials.

The final certificate is the Safety Equipment certificate which is issued for 2 years subject to an inspection and endorsement after one year. This certificate refers to the life saving equipment, life boats, and life rafts as well as portable fire fighting equipment.
It also details the maximum number of crew and passengers which may be carried under normal circumstances.

An agent should ensure that if the vessel accepts bookings for passengers including supercargoes and driver accompanying vehicles on RoRo vessels or is used for repatriating crew from other vessels, the maximum number allowed by the safety equipment certificate is not exceeded.

The SOLAS regulations are not necessarily applicable to all sizes of vessels but those vessels to which they do not apply in full or part will be issued with an exemption certificate detailing to what extent the regulations are not applicable to the vessel in question. There are also differences between the certificates issued to passenger and cargo vessels. Full details of the requirements necessary for the issue of any of the above certificates can be found in the SOLAS regulations published by IMO. The latest edition is dated 1997 and is published in several languages. The application of SOLAS regulations will also depend upon the age of the vessel and the areas in which it trades. It is not unknown for over zealous officials to detain or fine vessels for breaches of regulations which do not actually apply to the vessel in question. All vessels are obliged to carry a copy of the SOLAS regulations and the master should be aware of those sections which apply to his ship. In case of query it is advisable for agents to have their own copy of the rules as those on the ship may be in a foreign language.

The unpredictable nature of shipping will often find a vessel with certificates near to, or beyond their expiry date, at ports where renewal may be impractical or undesirable. SOLAS regulations recognise this problem and allow limited extensions of up to 5 months under the authority of the flag state administration. In practice this is usually done by a consul or classification body endorsing the certificate subject to the vessel calling at a port more convenient or in its flag state and the certificate being renewed within the extended period.

When a vessel continues trading with an extended certificate it should be noted that they cannot be further extended without a full survey of the items covered by the certificate.

Port State Control inspectors may detain the vessel until such time as an expired certificate is renewed or extended.

In order to avoid delays to the vessel the agent should always check the expiry date of all certificates necessary to obtain clearance as soon as possible after arrival and certainly before they are presented to Customs. If any of the certificates need extending this can be put into progress immediately so as to allow the necessary extensions to be obtained in good time. Inspectors finding an expired certificate may insist upon making a second inspection to confirm the extention, as this second inspection will be charged for, the agent who anticipates the problem , may save his principal additional expenses.

The miscellaneous certificates produced to customs are also of interest to PSC inspectors. The loadline certificate could more properly be considered as a safety document in so far as it details the maximum safe draught to which a vessel can load given the type of cargo, geographical location and time of the year.

INTERNATIONAL LOAD LINE CERTIFICATE

INTERNATIONAL LOAD LINE CERTIFICATE (1966)

Issued under the provisions of the International Convention on Load Lines, 1966 under the authority of the Government of the

REPUBLIC OF MALTA

_by_ **Germanischer Lloyd**

Name of Ship	Distinctive number or letters	Port of Registry	Length (L) a defined in Article
" DANA "	9 H 4 8 1 1	Valletta	74.57 m

Freeboard assigned as:
* { A new ship
* { ~~An existing ship~~

* Delete whatever is inapplicable.

Type of Ship:
* ~~Type "A"~~
* Type "B"
* ~~Type "B" with reduced freeboard~~
* ~~Type "B" with increased freeboard~~

Freeboard from deck line   _Load Line_

Tropical	995	mm (T)	110	mm above
Summer	1105	mm (S)	Upper edge of line through center of	
Winter	1215	mm (W)	110	mm below
Winter North Atlantic	1265	mm (WNA)	160	mm below

Note: Freeboards and load lines which are not applicable need not be entered on the certificate.

Allowance for fresh water for all freeboards   110   mm.

The upper edge of the deck line from which these freeboards are measured is   0   mm   above/below _top of the freeboard (1st)_   deck at side.

This certificate is valid only for the "Restricted International Service" (M) according to the Society's Rules for Classification.

Date of initial or periodical survey   20th June, 1994

THIS IS TO CERTIFY that this ship has been surveyed and that the freeboards have been assigned and load lines a above have been marked in accordance with the International Convention on Load Lines, 1966.

This Certificate is valid until   19th June, 1999   , subject to periodical inspe in accordance with Article 14(1)(c) of the Convention.

Issued at   Hamburg   on   25th August, 1994

The undersigned declares that he is duly authorized by the said Government to issue this Certificate.

Germanischer Lloyd

Schreiter   Höppner

Notes:

1. When a ship departs from a port situated on a river or inland waters, deeper loading shall be permitted corresponding to the wel fuel and all other materials required for consumption between the point of departure and the sea.

2. When a ship is in fresh water of unit density the appropriate load line may be submerged by the amount of the fresh water allowance above. Where the density is other than unity, an allowance shall be made proportional to the difference between 1.025 and the actual densi

3 745 - 1987

43

THIS IS TO CERTIFY that at a periodical inspection required by Article 14(1) (c) of the Convention, this sl found to comply with the relevant provisions of the Convention.

Place.. Date..

.... Surveyor to Germanischer Lloyd
           (Signature)

Place.. Date..

.... Surveyor to Germanischer Lloyd
           (Signature)

Place.. Date..

.... Surveyor to Germanischer Lloyd
           (Signature)

Place.. Date..

.... Surveyor to Germanischer Lloyd
           (Signature)

The provisions of the Convention being fully complied with by this ship, the validity of this Certificat accordance with Article 19 (2) of the Convention, extended until..

Place.. Date..

.... Surveyor to Germanischer Lloyd
           (Signature)

ARTICLE 14(1) (c): A periodical inspection within three months either way of each annual anniversary date Certificate, to ensure that alterations have not been made to the hull or superstructures which would affect the calci determining the position of the load line and so as to ensure the maintenance in an effective condition of fittir applicances for:

      (i) protection of openings;

      (ii) guard rails;

      (iii) freeing ports; and

      (iv) means of access to crew's quarters.

РОССИЙСКИЙ МОРСКОЙ РЕГИСТР СУДОХОДСТВА
RUSSIAN MARITIME REGISTER OF SHIPPING

МЕЖДУНАРОДНОЕ СВИДЕТЕЛЬСТВО
О ПРЕДОТВРАЩЕНИИ ЗАГРЯЗНЕНИЯ НЕФТЬЮ
INTERNATIONAL OIL POLLUTION PREVENTION CERTIFICATE

Выдано в соответствии с положениями Международной конвенции по предотвращению загрязнения с судов 1973 г., изм

Протоколом 1978 года к ней*, по уполномочию Правительства _____
Российским Морским Регистром судоходства   (название государства)

Issued under the provisions of the International Convention for the Prevention of Pollution from Ships, 1973, as modified by the Pr

1978 relating thereto * under the authority of the Government of _____
by Russian Maritime Register of Shipping   (name of the State)

СВЕДЕНИЯ О СУДНЕ
PARTICULARS OF SHIP

Название судна Name of Ship	Регистровый номер или позывной сигнал Distinctive Number or Letters	Порт приписки Port of Registry	Валовая вместимость Gross Tonnage	Ном ИМ IM Num

Тип судна
Type of ship

нефтеналивное судно для перевозки нефти
oil tanker

судно, не являющееся нефтеналивным судном, с грузовыми танками, подпадающими под дей
правила 2 (2) Приложения I к Конвенции
ship other than an oil tanker with cargo tanks coming under regulation 2 (2) of Annex I of the Convention

судно, не являющееся ни одним из перечисленных выше
ship other than any of the above

Примечание. Настоящее Свидетельство должно дополняться Описанием конструкции и оборудования.
Note.   This Certificate shall be supplemented by the Record of Construction and Equipment.

НАСТОЯЩИМ УДОСТОВЕРЯЕТСЯ:
THIS IS TO CERTIFY:

1. Что судно освидетельствовано в соответствии с правилом 4 Приложения I к Конвенции.
   That the ship has been surveyed in accordance with regulation 4 of Annex I of the Convention.

2. Что освидетельствованием установлено, что конструкция, оборудование, системы, арматура, устрой
   материалы судна и их состояние во всех отношениях удовлетворительны, а также что судно о
   применимым к нему требованиям Приложения I к Конвенции.
   That the survey shows that the structure, equipment, systems, fittings, arrangements and material of the ship and the condition
   are in all respects satisfactory and that the ship complies with the applicable requirements of Annex I of the Convention.

* Далее — «Конвенция».
  Hereinafter referred to as "the Convention".
** Ненужное зачеркнуть.
   Delete as appropriate.

Настоящее Свидетельство действительно до "_____" _____при условии проведения освидетельст
в соответствии с правилом 4 Приложения I к Конвенции.

This Certificate is valid until "_____" _____ subject to surveys in accordance with regulation 4 of Annex I of the C

Выдано в
Issued at

(место выдачи Свидетельства)
(place of issue of Certificate)

(дата выдачи)
(date of issue)

Российский Морской Регистр Судоходства
Russian Maritime Register of Shipping

М.П.
L.S.

№

(подпись должным образом уполномоченного лица,
выдавшего Свидетельство)
(signature of duly authorized official issuing the Certificate)

ПОДТВЕРЖДЕНИЕ ЕЖЕГОДНЫХ И ПРОМЕЖУТОЧНЫХ ОСВИДЕТЕЛЬСТВОВАНИЙ
ENDORSEMENT FOR ANNUAL AND INTERMEDIATE SURVEYS

Настоящим удостоверяется, что при освидетельствовании, требуемом правилом 4 Приложения I к
ции,установлено, что судно отвечает соответствующим положениям Конвенции.
This is to certify that at a survey required by regulation 4 of Annex I of the Convention, the ship was found to comply with th
provisions of the Convention.

Ежегодное освидетельствование
Annual Survey

Место
Place

Дата
Date

(штамп или печать полномочной организации)
(seal or stamp of the Authority, as appropriate)

(подпись должным образом уполномоченног
signature of duly authorized official)

Ежегодное/промежуточное* освидетельствование
Annual/Intermediate* Survey

Место
Place

Дата
Date

(штамп или печать полномочной организации)
(seal or stamp of the Authority, as appropriate)

(подпись должным образом уполномоченног
signature of duly authorized official)

Ежегодное/промежуточное* освидетельствование
Annual/Intermediate* Survey

Место
Place

Дата
Date

(штамп или печать полномочной организации)
(seal or stamp of the Authority, as appropriate)

(подпись должным образом уполномоченног
signature of duly authorized official)

Ежегодное освидетельствование
Annual Survey

Место
Place

Дата
Date

(штамп или печать полномочной организации)
(seal or stamp of the Authority, as appropriate)

(подпись должным образом уполномоченног
signature of duly authorized official)

_____
* Ненужное зачеркнуть.

CERTIFICATE OF CLASS

06886 –4
GL–Register–No.
GL–Register–Nr.

Hull
Schiff

—

This is to certify that the motor vessel
Hiermit wird bescheinigt, daß das Motorschiff

DANA

IMO–No. 7232652
IMO–Nr.

Port of Registry VALLETTA
Heimathafen

Flag REP. OF MALTA
Flagge

Call Sign 9H4811
U–Signal

Owner .... NORD–MED SHIPPING LTD.
Reeder

Shipyard .... MAGYAR HAJO– ES DARUGYAR ANGYALFÖLDI GYAREGYSEG
Schiffswerft

Place of Build BUDAPEST
Bauort

Launching 11.72
Stapellauf

Completion 7.73
Fertigstellung

has been surveyed at KILLINGHOME
besichtigt worden ist in

in 5.91
im

by our Surveyor
durch unseren Besichtiger

in accordance with this Society's Rules.
nach den Vorschriften dieser Gesellschaft.

Tonnage particulars acc. to Convention 69 acc. to International Tonnage Certificate (1969)
Vermessungsdaten des Schiffes nach Konvention 69 laut internationaler Schiffsmeßbrief (1969)

Gross Tonnage Bruttoraumzahl	1510	Length Länge	74,57 m	Summer Freeboard Sommerfreibord	1,105 m
Tonnage net Nettoraumzahl	763	Breadth Breite	11,30 m	with a mit einem	
		Moulded Depth Seitenhöhe	6,40 m	Moulded Draught Tiefgang ohne Kiel	5,307 m

On the basis of the Report submitted the vessel has been assigned the Class
Aufgrund des über den Befund erstatteten Berichtes ist dem Schiff die Klasse

with the Character of Class
mit dem Klassenzeichen

✠100A5 M (Restricted International Service) E
with freeboard 1,105 m

Strengthened for Heavy Cargo

and the Period of Class running from June 1991
und der Klassenlauf vom .... gerechnet erteilt worden.

Hamburg, 17th October 1995

Germanischer Lloyd

Förster ng

Jessen

This Certificate of Class is valid only in connection with 1–page ANNEX and all Certi–
ficate entries made by GL Surveyors on appended sheets in respect of this vessel's hull.
Dieses Klassenzertifikat ist nur gültig in Verbindung mit 1–seitigem Anhang und allen für dieses Schiff von GL–Besichtigern auf Beiblättern
erstellten Zertifikatseintragungen.

PORT AGENCY

Special Survey / Class Renewal

On the basis of the survey at (Place) ....

in (month and year) ....the Class ....

now running from .... has been renewed. ....   Stamp

Place .... Date .... Surveyor ....

On the basis of the survey at (Place) ....

in (month and year) .... the Class ....

now running from .... has been renewed. ....   Stamp

Place .... Date .... Surveyor ....

The present Certificate has been issued in compliance with the Classification and Construction Rules c
Germanischer Lloyd.

This is the reverse of the certificate on Page 47

Like the safety certificates the load line certificate is issued for a short time only (5 years) and subject to annual surveys in order to remain valid.

The Oil Pollution Prevention certificate is issued under Marpol 73/78 and ensures that vessels have effective means of preventing accidental pollution by oil and similar substances carried as fuel, lubricants or for other purposes but not as part of the cargo.

Other certificates and documents carried on board which will be of interest to the PSC inspector but not necessarily to the agent will include the following.

Classification Certificates. - detailing the class assigned to the vessel. It may contain details on restricted trading areas or other conditions which if contravened might allow action by PSC Inspectors.

Minimum Safe Manning Certificate - This carries a list of the number and qualifications needed for the officers and crew in order for the vessel to be considered safely manned. Usually it will detail alternative manning schemes if the vessel can be employed in short sea traffic as well as international trade. It will also mention if additional men of lower rank are permitted to replace one of a higher rank.

Grain Certificate - which details, methods and quantities of bulk grain which may be safely loaded on the vessel. Single hold vessels are not permitted to put to sea in a condition which would allow the cargo to shift and make the ship unstable. In practice this means that the hold must be completely full. Vessels which have several holds carrying part cargoes or cargoes for discharge at more than one port are permitted to leave some holds empty or only partially full. Exact details are contained within the vessel grain booklet.

Cargo Securing Manual - A book which details the fixed cargo securing points, portable securing equipment and details of how they are to be used. More importantly this manual will carry means of calculating the stresses and forces which securing equipment will be subjected to at different locations within the vessel. A cargo securing manual for general cargo ships became mandatory at the beginning of 1998. These manuals are normally endorsed by a Classification Society or government maritime officials.

Crew Competency Certificates - issued to officers and certain crew by maritime authorities detailing their rank, specialised training, and abilities. These certificates will take on much more significance with the full introduction of the S.T.C.W. Convention. This is an I.M.O. convention covering the Safety, Training and Certification of Watchkeepers. In essence it lays down minimum standards and qualifications which need to be attained by ships crew members as well as other matters such as hours of work and training.

Safety Management Certificates - These certificates are issued to ships in accordance with the ISM code. They are issued only after the safety management system of the ship operator has been fully investigated in the shore office and confirmed as being adhered to on board the ship. The ISM code is a determined attempt by the IMO to involve the shore based operators in the implementation of the SOLAS regulations and to develop their own systems to improve safety and reduce the risks of accident and pollution. Depending on the ship type SMCs will be introduced between 1998 and 2002. Some states including those in the E.U. have actually passed legislation to bring forward these dates for some types of ships.

Port State Control Inspection - The inspector is required to issue the vessel with his inspection report detailing any deficiencies and required action to be taken to remedy them. In the event of any detention or other penalty being imposed the inspector must inform the nearest representative of the flag state, usually a consulate or embassy. A further copy of the report is filed with the PSC directorate in St. Malo France, if the port involved is in a country operating PSC under the Paris memorandum. Reports are stored on computer and can be accessed by other states officials. This ensures that a vessel considered a safety risk can be followed and monitored by PSC officials in any port. Changing the name of the vessel will not conceal its past as all vessels are given a unique IMO number when first registered. This number stays with the ship all its life regardless of changes in ownership, flag or name.

In the event that the penalty or detention imposed upon a vessel is later found to have been unnecessary or unreasonable the PSC Inspectorate may have to pay damages to the owner of the vessel concerned. This can happen if the inspector has wrongly applied regulations which are not applicable to that ship for one reason or another.

Consuls and Embassies

The role of Consuls and Embassies with regard to the extention of certificates and PSC penalties has already been discussed.

Agents may also find the need to approach representatives of foreign governments when crew and or passengers desert, die or are hospitalised. Some states require vessels under their flag to lodge reports with consular officials whenever they arrive in a foreign port. Many flag states require ships logs and other ships records to be kept only in approved format documents. In the event that at an agent is requested to supply blank forms he should firstly check if the flag state does have any such requirements and may need to have blank forms stamped or otherwise endorsed by a consul before delivery to the vessel.

For vessels destined to certain countries, the USA for example, it may be necessary to obtain visas for crew and passengers at the last port of call outside that country, this will require the submission of visa applications and will usually be done by the agent.

There are many agency companies and individuals who, by virtue of attending ships of one country over many years, may be honoured by being appointed Consuls or Vice-consuls.

They will then be able to attend to some or all maritime matters on behalf of the government which has appointed them. They may additionally be permitted to charge for the issue of visas etc. thus gaining some financial advantage as well as prestige.

Coastguards

In the UK the coast guards role is mainly that of an emergency service during peacetime.

They will co-ordinate search and rescue operations and maintain monitoring services of marine traffic. Since 1995 they have also been the central point for the reporting of vessels carrying dangerous goods.

All shipowners are required to advise the Dover coast guard of any vessel calling at a British Port or navigating in British waters and carrying hazardous cargoes. They must also advise the coast guard of where, full information of the type, quantity, and stowage details of the cargo can be obtained in the case of an emergency. Although the onus is on the shipowner or operator to advise the coastguard and maintain the information required, this is usually done by the agent acting for the owner.

In other countries the role of the coastguard may be extended to cover activities such as policing, drug enforcement etc. The USA for example has a particularly vigorous and effective coastguard service with powers much greater than many of its European counterparts. There they are also responsible for Port State Control operations as well as being prime movers in drafting maritime legislation.

Other Government Departments.

In any country local regulations may well require the agent to deal with government departments which, at first glance may, have little to do with shipping.

Within the UK, there are several such departments which an agent may at some time come into contact with . As a rule maritime affairs are under the control of the Department of Environment, Transport and the Regions (DETR) but cargo matters may involve the Department (Board) of Trade and Industry (DTI) as certain commodities will require import or export licences issued by this department.

The Department of Trade also occasionally, produces statistics on port expenditure by foreign vessels. They may approach agents to provide details of incurred costs by vessels handled by them. These details are then collated and used to calculate the country's invisible earnings from foreign shipowners.

The protection of Britain's forests from foreign insect pests and diseases is delegated to the Forestry Commission. Any timber cargo from outside the E.U. is required to be accompanied by a phyto-sanitary certificate the absence of which may result in the cargo being refused discharge or ordered to be destroyed. Timber is widely used as dunnage or packing material and the Forestry Commission are enpowered to reject cargoes of any description where the timber used for these purposes is of a suspect quality.

Phyto-sanitary certificates are also required for other cargoes of plant material but these are usually subject to control by the Ministry of Agriculture Fisheries and Food (MAFF). This ministry also concerns itself with the environmental protection of British waters and will require full details of any emergency disposal of pollutants into coastal waters.

Plant health concerns are not limited to the U.K. since many countries have crops or other natural resources which may be severely affected by inadvertently imported pests. The agents role here is to inform owners of any restrictions at the earliest opportunity. Should the restriction only apply to ships which may have called to other ports or regions in a certain period the agent should explain the regulations fully so as to avoid expensive delays to the ship.

Forest and crops are not the only sensitive natural resources. Animals are also susceptible to diseases. When a government wishes to protect animals they may require veterinary certificates for live animals and animal products.

Any major incident involving ships in British waters or British ships abroad will be investigated by the Marine Accident Investigations Board (MAIB), a branch of the DETR. Most other countries have a similar body to investigate incidents in their own waters or concerning their own vessels. The results of these investigations and their recommendations are used by IMO in formulating new regulations or amendments to SOLAS.

PORT AGENCY

Chapter Three

THE AGENT AND PORT SERVICES

Port Facilities

The last chapter looked at the contact an agent has with authority but of course most of the services provided to ships are of a commercial nature and are therefore provided by independent contractors.

Ports or facilities within ports, fall into different categories of ownership and accountability. Some are state owned and operated, although this is becoming less common today. Some may be run by trusts established by national government but operating independently, others may be run by local government or municipal authorities or may be private. Some ports may have more than one governing body particularly those on rivers and estuaries. Here the jurisdiction is usually split between the port or dock and the river conservancy authority.

Whatever category a port falls into it will inevitably have rules and regulations laid down covering matters such as navigational procedures and restrictions, payment of dues and charges, and handling procedures and/or restrictions.

PORT AGENCY

Port authorities may also provide some or all of the ancillary services such as pilotage, towage, stevedoring etc., but this is not universal. In most ports such services are provided by independent private contractors.

When a vessel enters a port it will be required to pay dues of some description, usually conservancy harbours and/or light dues. These are paid to cover the upkeep of navigational aids such as buoys, light etc. and for any necessary dredging or other work needed to maintain the navigable channels.

Upkeep and maintainence of the docks and berths is usually included in a charge known variously as dock dues, berth dues, ship or port dues.

The basis for calculating these charges varies at least as much as the names they are given. It is quite common for the basis of charge to be either the nett or gross tonnage of the vessel although the deadweight is sometimes used. Alternatively the charge may be based on the length of the vessel, time spent on the berth or in the port, or the quantity of cargo handled. There are a number of ports which calculate dues on a volume basis obtained by multiplying the length, beam and draught of the vessel.

Such charges may be further complicated by differentials dependent upon the ports of origin or destination of cargoes, reductions for part cargoes or vessels taking cargo both in and out of the port, surcharges for vessels trading under flags of convenience and differentials for type of cargo being handled.

Whatever method and base of charging it is certain that some vessels appear to be charged excessively whilst others appear to pay hardly any dues. Of course any amendment to the basis of charging is certain to produce as many losers as winners.

Charges levied by Port Authorities are usually required to be paid before the vessel is permitted to sail, (see section on customs clearance) although a number of ports will extend credit to known agents or owners. In some cases ports will have bye-laws making the agent liable for charges in the event of the owner defaulting. It is important for agents to know and understand their liabilities and port bye-laws as ships dues can reach considerable sums.

Some ports may require the agent to sign an undertaking making themselves liable as principals, if the agent cannot be sure of his owner, principals intention or ability to pay he must weigh the risks of a lost agency against the possible liability and make his own decision.

An agent's dealing with the port authority is unlikely to be a mere financial transaction as he should be discussing navigational matters such as berthing, docking and manoeuvering with the harbour master or port captain. If the vessel is to berth at one of the port authorities facilities he will also need to check availability and suitability of the offered berth.

In the event that the vessel will have on board hazardous cargoes this will also have to be reported to the port authority. The procedure for reporting dangerous goods varies from port to port with some ports only accepting direct computer input. An agent must be aware of this before accepting an appointment as he may find it impossible to carry out his duties if he does not have the necessary computer links.

Pilots

Pilots are employed to assist the master in navigating the approaches to and the water inside ports. Vessels are most at risk of collision or stranding in these areas and therefore good knowledge of currents, depths and obstructions is of vital importance. Pilots may be employees of the port authority or they may be self-employed. In many ports use of a pilot is compulsory although exemptions may be granted for certain types of vessels or regular callers. Exemptions for regular callers apply generally to the master or other navigating officer and not the vessel itself.

Pilots are taken on board or leave the vessel at recognised pilot stations and will need some means of access to the vessel. The usual way is by one of an approved pilot ladder or hoist belonging to the ship, and required by SOLAS regulations. One of the major causes of Port State Control detentions or deficiency reports is the lack of a suitable pilot ladder.

Pilots will normally require good notice of a vessels ETA and any amendments that may be made. This allows the pilotage authority to ensure that a pilot is on station ready to assist the vessel. Late orders mean that a pilots time may have been wasted waiting for a vessel in vain or a pilot having to be called out at short notice. When timing is critical, for example in a tidal port, the agent must maintain an up to the minute monitoring of the vessels movements.

Failure to provide proper notice may result in a surcharge of up to 50% of the final bill.

The agent will often need to confirm when a vessel arrives at the pilot station in order to submit a notice of readiness in accordance with the Charter Party. On sailing the agent will need to book an outward pilot some hours before actual sailing otherwise service may not be guaranteed and the vessel delayed accordingly.

Where a port has more than one pilot station and regulations limiting use of each to vessels of a certain size or routing, the agent must ensure that proper information as to which station to use is given to the vessel in good time.

Many ports operate a system where a second person usually referred to as a steersman or helmsman is employed to assist the pilot. It is also common for dock, river-canal and berthing pilots to be used in addition to the sea pilot and charged for separately. Frequently these services will be provided by a different organisation than the sea pilot. There are a number of ports where pilots are self-employed and a shipowner may prefer to make use only of one or two individuals who are known to him and experienced in the handling of his vessel. In ports where this system operates it is important for the agent to check with owners beforehand, particularly if they are being appointed for the first time.

Pilotage charges are based upon many different criteria. Usually the length and draught are taken into consideration along with either the gross or nett tonnage. Often the distance the vessel has been piloted is the major basis of pilotage charges. Occasionally the time spent in piloting the vessel is as an hourly based charge.

Pilotage exemptions are very attractive to shipowners in ports where charges for this service are high. The agent will need to provide the owner with the proper application forms along with copies of any harbour bye-laws, regulations and navigating instructions. Masters and navigating officers on small vessels will probably only need to prove a number of passages with a pilot on board to be granted exemption. Their counterparts on larger vessels may have to pass an examination before being granted the same privilege. Even if a vessel is known to be exempt from compulsory pilotage the agent should check that no pilot is required. Changes in ships personnel and weather conditions may mean the vessel requires professional assistance.

Towage

With the advent of bow thrusters and modern steering aids port towage has become less important than when ships in port were difficult to manoeuver and likely to become involved in collisions or strandings. However for large vessels or even smaller ships in busy ports, towage may be desirable or even compulsory.

Before ordering tugs the agent must, unless towage is

compulsory, make all efforts to receive owners or masters confirmation as to the size and number of tugs required. This is important as towage costs are one of the most expensive items incurred at a port. Furthermore many masters will receive bonuses for working without tugs, or penalties for employing too many, unless exceptional circumstances prevail.

When tugs have been ordered the agent must continually monitor and advise the tug company of any changes in the time when towage will be required. Most tug companies charge up to 50% for baulk services ordered and not used, even if they subsequently perform the work.

Another point which needs to be checked is whether or not extra charges are made for use of the tugs ropes, and if such charges are applied whether or not they were justified. Towage outside of normal hours may be prohibitively expensive and all agents should advise owners of the extra costs involved. When the vessel is not scheduled to begin immediate work the owner may decide to anchor off and berth at a time when costs are less expensive.

Mooring and Unmooring

The act of making a ship fast to, or releasing from the berth is performed either by shore personnel, by boatman or by ships crew depending upon size of vessel and circumstances.

Whenever this operation is done by persons other than those permanently stationed on a berth or other facility it is important that the agent makes arrangements to ensure that the mooring or unmooring gang are at the correct place at the correct time.

Generally mooring or unmooring a vessel is a relatively straightforward operation with lines being passed ashore from the vessel, either directly or by use of a mooring boat. The shore man will then attach the ropes to the correct mooring points.

Mooring or unmooring by ships crew is permitted in some ports but strictly prohibited in others. The agent needs to make his principal aware in either case so that relevant instructions may be passed on to the master.

The exact times of events in mooring should be recorded as some charter parties may attach importance to "first line ashore" or "all fast".

Stevedores

The main reason for a call of a cargo vessel to a port will be for the purpose of loading or discharging a cargo. Since this is the province of the stevedores the agents relationship with them can be of vital importance.

The agent needs to be aware of the terms of which the cargo is carried as this will determine who will be called upon to order and pay for the cargo handling operations.

When a cargo is under either 'free in' or 'free out' terms the stevedoring will be arranged by the charterer's, shipper or receiver. In this case the agent needs to keep interested parties fully informed as to the ships arrival and readiness for working. He will also deliver to the stevedore any stowage plans, manifests or copy bills of lading necessary for the stevedore to properly identify what cargo is to be loaded or discharged and where in the vessel it is, or will be, located.

For cargoes carried under terms which call for the shipowner to arrange and pay for stevedoring the agent can take a much more active role. He must be prepared to negotiate with the stevedore in order to secure for owners a reasonable cost for the handling, and, if there is a choice of stevedores, to select the best equipped and skilled for the job in hand. Some cargoes require special expertise in handling and it is of no use to opt for a stevedore with cheap rates if they are unused to that cargo and cause damage resulting in claims against the owner.

PORT AGENCY

In ports where the port authority have a cargo handling operation there may be some advantage in negotiating 'all in' rates for port dues and stevedoring combined. Agents who frequently act for ships of different owners carrying similar cargoes may be able to negotiate competitive rates by using the total cargo capacity as a bargaining point. If successful the agent will not only please the shipowners but is likely to attract appointments from other shipowners wishing to take advantage of the lower costs.

Agents who have such relationships with stevedores need to be careful not to lose sight of the fact that their prime consideration must be to protect the owners interest. Therefore in the event of any complaint from the ship against the stevedore they must be prepared to present the owners case, even if this results in some souring of relationships between the stevedores and agent.

When discussing stevedoring operations with a shipowner the agent should be fully conversant with the normal methods at loading and discharging ports. For example problems may occur when loading bulk cargoes where no manual trimming is available if the vessel is of a type that is not self-trimming or able to be otherwise mechanically trimmed, or if shore cranes do not have the capacity required to move cargo loaded elsewhere, especially if the ship concerned is gearless. When discussing Ro Ro vessels the position and type of the ships ramp may be an issue that needs to be resolved before the vessel is accepted. In the event that the agent is being consulted prior to completing the fixing of the vessel he will almost certainly be asked about the likely speed of loading or discharging. This information will be used to determine details in the charter party relevant to laytime, despatch and demurrage.

Once a cargo is discharged from a vessel the owner may have little control over it and its eventual delivery to the receiver. Many charter parties and bills of lading give the owner the right of lien for freight, dead freight, demurrage or other charges payable by cargo interests. It is therefore important for the agent to advise the owner what will be the stevedores probable position, in allowing the owner to exercise this right.

Apart from the cost of physically moving cargo to or from the ships holds there are normally other ancillary operations which may be carried out by stevedores, riggers or the ships crew. These may involve trimming, stowing, dunnaging, lashing or unlashing and hatch sealing. Under a charter party some of those expenses may be for a different account than those for cargo handling. The agent should enquire as soon as possible as to the liabilities for these services and be ready to order them from other contractors if they are not to be performed by stevedores. When advising owners and others of stevedoring costs it will be necessary to mention which, if any, charges are included.

Tallying

The practice of unitising cargo in containers or on trailers has effectively reduced the need to employ tally clerks for cargo carried by these methods. There are still however many cargoes for which careful tallying is required.

Most stevedores will provide a count of cargo being handled by them but this count may not be undertaken at a time or place satisfactory to the owners. For cargoes to be loaded a stevedores count will often take place on delivery of the cargo to the port by road or rail transport. This may be several days before the arrival of the ship and there is therefore plenty of opportunity for part of the cargo to be 'lost' within the port system. Providing the ships crew makes a diligent check on the number of pieces actually loaded any difference can be checked before signing of the Bill of Lading and problems can therefore be avoided. The situation for discharged cargoes is similar but if any cargo is 'misplaced' before delivery to receivers, often many days after the vessel sails, the owner may well face claims for shortages. Ideally tallying of discharged cargoes should take place alongside the ship during discharge and any shortages brought to the attention of the master so that investigations can be started as to the location of the missing cargo. Tallies will also bring to light overlanded cargo which may belong to previous or subsequent ports of call or shipped in excess of declared quantity. The owner may then have established a right to extra freight.

PORT AGENCY

The conditions applying to port tallies should be advised by the agent to the owner who can then make an informed decision as to the need for additional protective measures.

Some receivers of cargo may operate a non-tally system whereby the ship owner does not employ independent tally clerks but instead pays a fixed amount to the receiver who then waives his right to make claims against the shipowner for shortages.

Apart from recording the quantity of cargo loaded or discharged the tally report will also detail any obviously damaged or badly marked cargo.

Surveyors

Sometimes it is necessary to have a more detailed report than is provided by a ships tally.

This may be because the cargo being carried is liable to be damaged easily by any variety of means, some of which are outside the shipowners control. For example paper on rolls is prone to damage by chafing movements in the ship, by crushing, or by mishandling on shore.

When it is difficult for the ships cargo officers to identify pre-shipment damage at the loading port, inspection by a more experienced specialist may reveal defects which can be noted and agreed before the voyage begins. During discharge the surveyor may well notice damage being caused by the stevedores which if not brought to everybody's attention may later be claimed as ships damage. Some cargoes are so prone to problems that surveys are insisted upon by the shipowners or their P & I clubs. Steel is one such cargo which may surprise those not regularly engaged in its carriage.

When loading bulk cargoes a draught survey may be made to confirm or otherwise the claimed loaded quantity declared by the port or shippers. Draught surveys involve quite complex calculations involving what quantities of fuel, ballast and waste products are on board and where in the vessel they are located. The density of the water at the berth must also be taken into account.

Cargo and draught surveys are often carried out by two surveyors one on behalf of the owner and one appointed by the cargo interests. An agent who has not been asked to arrange a survey on behalf of the ship should always inform the owner if he discovers that cargo interests intend to make their own survey.

There are a number of cargoes which require the ships holds to be specially prepared. In such cases it is normal for the cargo interests to survey the ship before loading commences. Cargoes which require exceptionally clean holds include china clay, potash and petroleum coke.

Shipchandlers

The next chapter deals with supplies to the ship in more detail but it should be mentioned that unless there is a very good reason the agent should always leave the choice of shipchandler to the master. Most ships today operate with a fixed budget for stores and provisions which is controlled by the ship's officers. It is therefore better for them if they have a choice of competitive suppliers rather than being faced with a monopoly situation. The agent can also be blameless in the event that poor quality goods are supplied.

General Considerations

Whereas most of the official formalities are free of charge commercial services by their very nature involve costs, sometimes quite considerable sums. Agents should always make sure that when any service or supply is ordered they make it perfectly clear to the supplier that they are acting only as agents and give to them full details of the owner or other party responsible and liable for payment.

PORT AGENCY

Chapter Four

THE AGENT AND THE SHIP

Introduction

The previous two chapters covered the various formalities and commercial aspects connected with moving a vessel and cargo into or out of a port. There remains to be considered the requirements and needs of the vessel and its crew. This work is generally referred to as 'husbandry'. When a vessel is operating under time charter husbandry is undertaken on behalf of the ship owner unlike the port formalities and cargo services which are for the time charterers account. Although bunker supplies will be for time charterers account under most circumstances.

Husbandry services provided to a ship can be divided into two categories, namely services to the vessel itself and services connected with the ships crew.

Services to the ship

Bunkers

This has already been mentioned as a possible time charterers cost but whichever party is responsible for payment the agents duties are the same.

PORT AGENCY

When the agent is asked to order bunkers for the vessel he must first of all ensure that he knows exactly what grade and type of fuel is required. Modern ships use a variety of different fuels ranging from heavy fuel oil which is almost identical to crude oil, through a number of refined or semi-refined products to gas oil which is a highly refined diesel type fuel. Aside from the fuel type the amount of impurities particularly sulphur content may make a particular fuel unsuitable for certain vessels. The agent should never make the mistake of ordering fuel for a vessel based on a previous supply to a sister ship since there is always the possibility that the vessels may have different types of engines.

The majority of ships are able to use an alternative fuel in the event that the preferred type is not available but orders should only be made after checking with the owner or chief engineer on board. Apart from the main engine all vessels are required to have on board emergency generators and many vessels also have other ancillary engines providing power to different equipment on the vessel. These small engines normally run on diesel or gas oil and will require supplies of fuel possibly different to that of the main engine.

Having ascertained the quantity and type of fuel needed the agent will need to co-ordinate delivery taking into account possible restrictions with regard to time and place of delivery. Some ports will not permit delivery of bunkers during cargo handling operations others may not permit delivery by road tanker at any time. When ordered in large quantities bunkers are usually delivered by barge, the cost of which may or may not be included in the quoted price. The agent must be aware of this and any other hidden costs such as port dues on bunkers taken by vessels. The speed at which bunkers can be delivered to the vessel should be taken into account as this may affect the time the vessel will be ready for departure.

With regard to price of bunkers the agent should if possible obtain quotes from different suppliers, and at all times should pass on offers of alternative grades so that the owner can make an informed decision as to which fuel may be more economic.

When bunkers are ordered directly by the owner the agent must still be prepared to co-ordinate the delivery as above.

Bunkers may be purchased either from major oil companies, through stockholders or via brokers. There are a number of specialist bunker brokers whose price may well be lower than those offered by direct suppliers.

Closely allied to bunkers and ordered in the same manner are lubricating oils (Lubes) and fuel additives. These are relatively much more costly than bunkers but usually only ordered in small quantities and delivered in drums by lorries.

Lubes and additives may well have proprietary names but again suitable alternatives are generally offered by all of the main suppliers.

Ships Spares and Repairs

The increasing use of technology on board ships together with the ever increasing sophistication of navigational aids, engine monitoring systems and engines themselves has made on board running repairs more difficult and impractical today. The fact that the vessel requires most of its equipment to be operational in order to satisfy class requirements and international regulations means that any defective equipment must be replaced or repaired without undue delays. The ship will under most circumstances communicate his needs to his owner whilst at sea. The owner may then request the agent to investigate the possibility of obtaining spares or repairs locally or he may make his own arrangements to deliver any spares needed to the agent, or to make direct order for a service company to attend the vessel.

In the event that spares are sent by the owner it will be the agents responsibility to arrange collection and delivery to the ship on arrival. Spares may require to be customs cleared at the point of entry into the agents country. When spares arrive by air the airport may be too far distant for the agent to arrange customs clearance himself and he will need to use the services of a clearing agent or freight forwarder. Small items may be delivered prior to vessels arrival to the agent's office but large heavy items will need to be delivered direct to the ship. The agent needs to be aware of the size and weight to make his arrangements accordingly.

When the agent is asked to locate spares he will undoubtedly be asked by potential suppliers for full details of the type and specification of the items in question. In order to answer these queries promptly the agent will have had to gather as much information from the master and owners as possible beforehand. Particular care should be exercised in checking the information supplied. Some machinery including main engines may exist in two versions, one with metric measurements and the other with imperial, spare parts for one version will be useless for the other.

The agent will also need to know if fitting of spares can be performed by the crew or if a service engineer will need to attend to this matter. In common with all supplies to a vessel the agent should, whenever possible obtain quotes from different suppliers before ordering. Most agents will have built up a small library of catalogues and brochures of suppliers, manufacturers and their representatives which will help him in deciding which to approach for specific items.

Repairs can be more difficult to arrange because they usually require the attendance of a representative of the repairer to attend the vessel in order to assess time, cost and feasibility of any repair. When vessels have only a very limited stay in port such inspection should be arranged to take place as soon as possible after arrival. It is not uncommon for the agent to need to make arrangements for inspections to take place at an anchorage on the roads if the vessel is not able to berth immediately upon arrival.

Repairs to the vessel involving any risk of fire or explosion such as welding or cutting or the risk of pollution must be discussed with the port authority and permission to undertake repairs obtained from the appropriate authority before commencement. If the vessel will be without power or disabled in any way during repairs the port may demand that work is done only at a designated repair berth, thus not preventing normal working for other arrivals to the port.

When repairs are made to any vessel or its equipment the agent will need to know if any survey or certification of the repair is necessary and make arrangements to ensure that these are indeed carried out and reports and certificates delivered to the next port if they were not ready in time.

The time taken for any repairs or delays due to repairs and waiting for spares must always be recorded by the agent as they can have a significant effect on laytime calculations in voyage charter parties and for vessels under time charters may require the vessel to be placed 'off hire' for part or all of the lost time.

Stores and Provisions

The term stores does not refer to foodstuffs but covers items supplied to the deck and engine compartments of the ship and not regarded as fixtures and fittings of the vessel.

Deck stores will cover such things as flags, charts, paints, ropes and cargo securing equipment etc. Common to both departments will be protective clothing, torches, spare bulbs for lamps etc. Most of the items mentioned will be obtainable from a general shipchandler but others may require sourcing from specialist suppliers. Some of the items such as charts and torches for use in emergencies may be required in order for the vessel to comply with international regulations. The charts on board must be kept upto date and in order to assist in this regard most governments produce 'Notices to Mariners'. Published weekly as small booklets they are obtainable free or at minimal cost from chart suppliers or customs offices. Agents should always have a stock of recent issues to place on board vessels they are attending.

71

PORT AGENCY

Provisions are the foodstuff for the crew of the vessel and must be carried in sufficient quantity to allow for the voyage to at least the next port to be completed without the risk of being used up.

Provisions will again be supplied in most instances by a shipchandler, although some crews prefer instead to obtain their own supplies from local markets.

On a large number of vessels crew victualling costs are fixed by agreement at a set sum per person per day. The ships cook will require to see price lists from different chandlers in order to secure for the crew the best quality and choice of provisions at the lowest costs taking into consideration the agreed daily rate. The agent may be able to assist the crew to improve this standard of provisions if he has knowledge of, and access to, local wholesale suppliers.

Occasionally a ship may request the agent to organise provisions in advance, particularly if the stay in port is likely to be of very short duration. This should present the agent with no problems although it will be advisable to check if the crew have special requirements due to cultural traditions or religious convictions.

All vessels are required to carry a certain amount of medical supplies on board for routine and emergency use. Items such as bandages or simple drugs like aspirin can be obtained from shipchandlers or local stores. There are however some drugs and medical equipment which can normally only be obtained under prescription. These items should be ordered from specialist ships pharmacist suppliers who will have the necessary licence to deliver to ships.

Fresh Water

Fresh water is of course essential on board any vessel and is normally available in most ports. Supply of fresh water may be by way of direct piped connection or by barge or road tanker. Whichever method is used the agent should have some idea of the speed at which water can be delivered, this is particularly important when dealing with large passenger ships which may require many hundreds of tonnes.

The cost of water supplies varies tremendously from port to port, so the agent should always indicate the cost when accepting an agency appointment. If there is any doubt as to the quality of the water the master may require a sample to be taken before delivery of the ordered quantity. Should the agent be aware of any likely contamination he must always advise the ship of his concerns.

Waste Removal

In the days of wooden sailing ships very little waste was produced on board vessels other than galley waste and sewage. Ballast voyages were usually made with holds loaded with stone, sand or bricks. Today with the advent of mechanical propulsion and the use of water ballast large amounts of oily waste will accumulate in the ship.

This was not considered a problem in less enlightened times with the waste being dumped at sea. Today's concern with pollution has seen the introduction of the Maritime Pollution (MARPOL) international conventions and regulations designed to prevent this practice. Although disposal at sea of some garbage and sewage is still permitted, ships must now retain certain types of garbage, solid and dirty liquid waste on board until they reach a port with facilities for proper disposal.

The facilities required to be arranged depend upon the type of waste which the ship wishes to dispose of.

PORT AGENCY

Dry waste such as galley waste, unwanted dunnage and general rubbish will be put into skips provided by the port or ordered from an outside contractor. There is usually only a small charge made for this service unless the quantities are unusually high as for example a large passenger ship. When dunnage or separation materials are being disposed of the agent may know of a local contractor who will be prepared to buy them. Such offers are of course very welcome to the owner.

Liquid waste containing oil residues is usually stored in special tanks within the ship until sufficient quantities have been accumulated to make disposal economically viable. Disposal is usually into a specialists contractors barges or road tankers. Facilities for disposal of this type of waste do not exist in all ports and where they do they can be prohibitively expensive. This is surprising since oily waste can be recycled to produce valuable oil products. The same cannot be said of sewage waste which also has to be disposed of from time to time.

Fines for improper disposal of waste are increasing rapidly in an attempt to deter ships from illegal discharges. Apart from the fines the shipowner may find himself liable for clean up operations and compensation. It is not unexpected therefore to note that owners have become much more aware of the benefits of properly disposing of waste from their ships. In the EU directives have been issued making the shoreside disposal of some types of waste compulsory.

Ships Certificates

The main certificates which a ship needs to carry and produce at customs have already been discussed at length in earlier chapters. There are however several more certificates which although not needed for customs purposes need to be kept up to date. More importantly the equipment they cover needs to be operating satisfactorily and maintained in good condition. The owner or master will generally advise the agent in advance of any certificates near to their expiry date and request the agent to make the necessary arrangements for certificates to be renewed or extended. This will most likely involve a survey by the vessels classification society or a specialist supplier or contractor.

Examples of the types of equipment which are often certificated include fire extinguishers, survival suits, breathing apparatus, cargo securing and handling gear, lifeboat stores, pyrotechnics and the lifeboats themselves. Any expired certificate may result in Port State Control penalties, it is therefore important for the agent to inform the owners if any requested survey is impossible to arrange.

The Ships Crew

Seamen have always needed to be resourceful people and even if their work has become a little easier this is still true today. They also tend to have an international grapevine along which useful information on all ports is passed from seaman to seaman. Even so an agent should be able to advise crew members on bus and train times and costs, places to avoid, and places of interest. He may if there is time arrange sightseeing tours or sporting competitions for the crew. Some ports hold annual seamans sport weeks open to any visiting seafarers. Most ports have some form of club where crews meet other seaman and relax with their own kind.

It is always a good idea for the agent to produce a few pages of information about the port and shopping or other facilities available nearby. This can be put on board on arrival and is usually much appreciated by the crew.

Occasionally the agent will need to take a deeper interest in crew welfare and will need to be able to respond to medical and other emergencies.

Sick and Injured Seamen

In the event that a seaman requires medical attention on arrival the agent will have to arrange a visit to a doctor, dentist or hospital. Injuries, major illnesses, and events such as heart attacks or strokes obviously require attention but if a seaman is suspected of having a contagious disease the port health authorities must be informed and their instructions followed at all times.

When arranging medical attention the agent should inform the doctor or person attending that the patient is a seaman, and also the seamans nationality and the flag of his ship. This information is necessary as some countries will not charge for medical attention if special arrangements exist between them and the seaman's or ship's home country.

Should a seaman become seriously ill or injured at sea prior to arrival or shortly after sailing it may be necessary to arrange helicopter evacuation. This is generally done by the medical authority or by coastguards although the agent may be instrumental in passing on the information.

When a crewman requires hospitalization and remains after his vessel has sailed the agent needs to closely monitor the crewman's situation. He should have taken off the seaman's passport and other personal belongings likely to be needed by the crewman during his stay and eventual repatriation. Bearing in mind the fact that the seaman may be foreign and unable to speak the local language the agent should attempt to obtain as much medical history as possible from the master, other crew and the shipowners. It is also important to know the religion, if any, of the patient as this may well affect the types of treatment which are acceptable, or should the matter end tragically the rites which need to be administered. In addition to these considerations the agent must inform the immigration officials and as a courtesy the consul or embassy of the home state of the crewman and the ship.

During the crewmans stay in hospital the agent should send regular reports to the owners and if possible the ship. He should also assist the crewman to make contact with relatives and friends if asked, and to obtain some reading material and creature comforts such as toiletries, fruit, spare clothes etc. It may be possible to arrange visitors from seaman's welfare organisations, other ships or from local people of the same nationality as the seaman. Of course if the patient objects to, or is distressed by such visits they should be stopped.

Deaths

Occasionally a seaman may succumb to illness, die from injuries received in an accident or commit suicide. The agent must then inform the local authorities and arrange for the removal of the body. If the death occurred under suspicious circumstances there will need to be some form of legal enquiry at which the agent may be required to attend on behalf of the ship. Deaths which occur in hospitals usually require a post mortem examination, if there is likely to be any objection to this on cultural or religious grounds the agent should inform the hospital and the consul or embassy of the deceased crewman, who will intervene at the highest level if necessary.

Undertakers must be employed to prepare the body for repatriation or burial. Once again cultural and religious traditions must be taken into account along with the official requirements of the countries involved and transporters of the body. Undertakers are usually fully aware of the official papers which need to accompany the body during repatriation and are quite prepared to attend to all formalities, although they may ask the agent to book and pay for sea or air transportation of the body.

Repatriations

Fortunately the vast majority of repatriations are of live persons, injured or healthy. Repatriation arrangements require immigration approval when the person concerned is a national of a country for which visas are required. A seaman may be repatriated for any of a variety of reasons. He may have been dismissed from the vessel, he may have completed his term of employment, he may be ill or injured, required on board another vessel or being repatriated on compassionate grounds. Except when a seaman has been dismissed the repatriation costs will under most circumstances be for the shipowners account. Dismissed seaman are, under most employment contracts, responsible for their own repatriation costs. Immigration laws however often make the agent responsible for all costs incurred if the owner or seaman refuses or is unable to pay. It is therefore in the agents own interest to obtain advance funds from the owner or seaman before making expensive arrangements.

When repatriating sick or injured seamen the agent should inform the airline or other carrier of the nature and extent of the illness or injury. This is particularly important if special attention or assistance is required during the journey. Severely disabled persons may need a medical escort to accompany them. Such escorts can be arranged either by hospitals or by commercial organisations specialising in air ambulance, and medical services.

What ever the reason for a repatriation the agent must make adequate arrangements for delivering the crew member to the airport or station and ensuring his departure on the correct flight or service. The ship owners may request the agent to advance a small amount of money to the seaman for use during the journey. The best agents will always ensure that any returning seaman has at least enough money for meals and refreshments whether the owner has provided it or not.

Crew Arriving

The mechanics in dealing with crew arriving to take up positions on board are much the same as for crew being repatriated. There may be one additional complication in that whereas crew being repatriated have been granted right to enter a country merely by virtue of being a crew member of a vessel, crew arriving may have to convince immigration officials of their intentions and rights to join a vessel. Occasionally crew arriving may not be in posession of the required documents. In such cases the agent must be ready to assist and explain to immigration the reasons why usual formalities could not be followed. An example would be when an officer or crewman essential under minimum safe manning regulations has been incapacitated or lost to the vessel for any reason and a replacement has to be found at extremely short notice.

Crew Mail and Ships Mail

Agents will usually be asked to despatch any mail either official or personal originating on the ship. They are of course entitled to recover any expenses they may incur in this regard, usually from the owner in the ships disbursement account. The owner will address to the agent any mail from his office for the ship and crew. When a vessel makes regular calls to a port a lot of personal mail for the crew will be sent care of the agent. In the event that mail arrives after the vessel sails the agent should forward it to an appropriate port or to the owners office.

Cash to Master

Agents are often requested to make cash advances to the master for crews wages and other uses on the vessel. The agent should always ensure that acceptable means of reimbursement are in place before paying over any cash. Where the sum involved is large it may be prudent to arrange for cash to be delivered by a security escort. The cost of this should be advised to the owner beforehand. It goes without saying that a receipt must always be obtained from the master when handing over any cash. Occasionally a master may return some cash on departure in which case the agent must issue his own receipt to the master, and credit the owner accordingly.

Chapter Five

CHARTER PARTIES

The Agent and the Charter Party

Unless a cargo is to be carried on a scheduled liner vessel it will be almost certain that the terms and conditions of the carriage will be enshrined in a charter party.

The charter party is agreed between shipowners and cargo interests either directly or more usually through brokers. Unless the agent is approached for advice by either of the parties during the negotiations he will have no opportunity to influence the actions of the parties involved.

We have already discussed the relationship between the agent, owners and charterers but it needs to be repeated that with very few exceptions the agent will always be the servant of the shipowner or operator. It is quite common to hear of the charterers agent but when talking of voyage charter parties this refers to the nomination and not the appointment. Unless the charter party clearly indicates that agents are to be appointed and paid by charterers the agent is legally obliged to act at all times in the best interests of the owner or operator.

Charter party forms and types are numerous and varied but from the agents point of view they fall into one of two very distinct categories namely time charters and voyage charters.

Time Charters

A time charter party will give the charterer the right to utilise the vessel as if he were the shipowner, subject to certain limitations with regard to types of cargo which may be carried and the intended trading areas.

The charterer may decide to operate the vessel as a liner or a tramp as he so wishes always providing he pays the hire money in accordance with the charter party. Most time charter parties also give the charterer the right to sub-let the vessel providing the sub charter party is back to back with the original.

Should the time charterer decide to operate the vessel on a tramp basis each voyage will be covered by a separate voyage charter entered into between the time charterer as the operator and the cargo interests as charterers.

When a vessel is operating under a time charter agreement the ship owner will remain responsible for crewing, repairing and maintaining the vessel, as well as arranging insurance cover for the ship but not the cargo. The appointment of port agents will be made by the time charterer but most time charter parties contain a clause under which the agent will be expected to attend to ships husbandry matters (see chapter 10) on behalf of the owner without any additional agency fee. There may of course be occasions when the work to be performed for the owner is above and beyond what might be considered normal. In such cases the owner will either agree to pay the charterer agent for this work or he may prefer to appoint another agent instead.

Under a bareboat or demise charter the shipowner hires the vessel alone to the charterer who then becomes responsible for all crewing, maintenance and repair. Agents acting for vessels which have been bareboat chartered will rarely, if ever, have any contact with the true owners.

Port agents may also be concerned with the time charter party terms at other times, specifically at redelivery on completion. Should the vessel be placed off hire at any time either for repairs, during arrests, or for any other reason the agent may be required to prepare off hire certificates or statements. These documents record the exact times when vessel is 'off hire' and the quantities of bunkers on board. This allows the time charter to reduce his hire payment for the vessel when it was not available to him and to charge for bunkers consumed during off hire periods.

During short periods off hire the charterer and the owner may mutually agree on times and bunker consumption. It is usual for the first on hire survey and the final off hire survey to be conducted by qualified surveyors who will record the condition of the vessel on each occasion.

When a vessel under time charter enters port the costs for port expenses such as pilots, tugs etc. are for the time charters account. Port Agents may be able to reduce these costs by bringing to the charterers attention any opportunities such as pilotage exemptions which the charterers can then request the owner to apply for.

Bareboat or demise charters also fall into this category but these types of charter parties are of very little interest to the port agent. They are merely forms of hire contracts between the owner of the vessel and the demise charterer. For practical purposes the agent can regard a demise charterer as the owner. The agent should be informed if a vessel consigned to him is operating under such a charter because he may need to separate some of the expenses.

Voyage Charters

Voyage charter parties are the most common form of contracts for the carriage of bulk cargoes. The majority of charter party forms today are of the box type with the first page being a series of boxes into which the details of the owners, charterers, ships cargo, the voyage and relevant dates and freight rates are entered. The second and subsequent pages being the text of the various clauses which cover the legal obligations, rights and responsibilities of each party. Agents will still encounter some of the older forms, which with their quaint type face and old fashioned paper sizes together with the style of language make them appear to be impressive if somewhat incomprehensible documents.

Given the effectiveness of modern communications it is perhaps surprising that many agents will not sight an actual charter party, but will instead be given only the barest details in the form a fixture recap. A fixture recap is usually produced by the owners or charterers broker and will refer to a standard C/P form e.g. Gencon or Nubaltwood. There then follows a string of detail written in broking terms and abbreviations. It is therefore important to learn, or at least have access to an up to date glossary of common abbreviations used in shipbroking practice.

The efficient agent will have blank copies of all standard forms as well as copies of any regularly encountered private C/P forms. This will enable him to fully understand the rights and responsibilities according to the contract terms if only a fixture recap is available.

The following tables details some of the more commonly encountered BIMCO approved charter parties.

DRY CARGOES

Cargo or Contract type	Full Charter Party name	Short name
Bareboat hire	BIMCO Standard Bareboat Charter	BARECON
Time charter	New York Produce Exchange	NYPE
Time charter	BIMCO Uniform time charter	BALTIME
Time charter	BIMCO Deep Sea time charter	LINERTIME
Coal	Americanised Welsh Coal charter	AMWELSH
Coal	BIMCO Coal voyage charter	POLCOLVOY
Coal	Japan Shipping Exchange Coal Charter Party	NIPPONCOAL
Grain	North American Grain Charter	NORGRAIN
Grain	Australian Wheat Charter	AUSTWHEAT

Grain	Continent Grain charter	SYNACOMEX
Grain	BIMCO Grain voyage charter	GRAINVOY
Timber	Chamber of Shipping Baltic wood charter party	NUBALTWOOD
Timber	Russian Wood Charter Party	RUSWOOD
Ore	Japan Shipping Exchange Iron Ore charter party	NIPPONORE
Ore	BIMCO Standard Ore charter party	OREVOY
Fertilisers	North American Fertiliser Charter Party	FERTIVOY
Fertiliser	Chamber of Shipping Fertilisers Charter Party	FERTICON
General purpose	BIMCO Uniform General Charter	GENCON
General purpose	BIMCO Scandinavian Voyage Charter	SCANCON

LIQUID CARGOES

Cargo or Contract type	Full Charter Party name	Short name
Time charter	INTERTANKO Tanker Time Charter Party	INTERTANKTIME
Oils	INTERTANKO Voyage Charter Party	TANKERVOY
Vegetable oils and fats	BIMCO Standard Voyage Charter Party for Vegetable/Animal oils and fats	BISCOILVOY
Chemicals	BIMCO Standard Voyage Charter Party for the Transportation of Chemicals in Tank Vessels	CHEMTANKVOY
Liquid gases	Gas Voyage Charter Party for Liquid Gas Except LNC	GASVOY

The above tables are not an exhaustive list of BIMCO approved forms and in addition there are countless numbers of forms which BIMCO do not approve as they consider them to be biased as well as a number of private forms. It is BIMCO's practice to suffix the short names with the year of the last amendment.

The Gencon Charter Party

The Gencon charter party was designed to cover those dry cargoes and trades for which no specific form was available. It has however come to be used more and more in trades for which it was not intended.

There are at least two reasons for this. Firstly because the original trade specific forms, have not evolved sufficiently to reflect the developments and changes within those trades. Secondly because of its popularity, many involved in chartering feel more comfortable with it than with forms which are used less frequently. It is however a relatively unsophisticated document and is hardly ever found unamended in some way.

Irrespective of the reason for which a Gencon is preferred it will need to have additional clauses drafted to cover items and practices not included in the main text. These additional clauses are frequently the root of disputes and costly legal proceedings, brought as a result of poor drafting and ambiguous wording, especially when they are drafted in a language other than the native tongue of the person drafting the clause, or are translated from other languages.

Unless the agent is also active in chartering his duties will only be to try to interpret these additional clauses and in case of doubts as to their intention, or where it is believed that they seriously threaten the owners interests to seek clarification and to advise the owner of what the agent sees as the consequences to the vessel and/or cargo at his port.

Almost all charter parties contain clauses to cover common operations, obligations, rights and responsibilities. Although the clauses in different charter party forms may be similar they are rarely identical. The agent needs to be alert to the differences between clauses in standard charter parties and also to look carefully at recaps or signed charters, to discover whether or not any alterations have been made.

A charter party will contain many clauses which are of no interest to the agent whatsoever. Other clauses will relate only to the loading or discharging operations and again these may have no bearing on the duties of the agent at the 'other end'.

An initial glance at a charter party will show that the clause regarding agency appointments is probably one of the shortest clauses in the charter party. This certainly does not mean that the agent is of little importance as a more detailed inspection will reveal that virtually every reference in the clauses to ' the owner' 'will be followed by' or his agent or representative 'or some similar wording.

In the event that anything does go wrong it will be the owner or charter who will have some liability as a result. The agent therefore needs to understand how a charter party is constructed, the reasons for different clauses and what might be required of him in order to satisfy the requirements of the charter party.

In order to illustrate these points let us consider the Gencon form in more detail.

The Gencon form was changed in 1974 from a text document to a box layout form. There have been some more recent amendments but we shall be using as a model the 1976 version.

The front page is quite easy to follow and needs little explanation. It will be noted that many of the boxes carry references to clauses in the text part of the form. Where such a reference is made the relevance will be examined when looking at the text part .

Boxes 1 to 5 identify the parties and the vessel as well as when and where the charter was concluded.

Box 6 refers to GT/NT, the vessels tonnage measurements.

Box 7 gives the maximum cargo tonnage the vessel can carry. This is only important if the cargo is 'deadweight' i.e. it has a stowage factor low enough to mean that the holds will not be full when the dwcc is reached.

Box 8 which gives the vessels present position might be of interest to the load port agent as it allows him to locate the current whereabouts and follow the vessel's progress to his port.

Box 9 is important as the date entered here will be the first on which the charterer is obliged to begin loading the ship provided it has arrived and is ready for loading. Sometimes a time as well as a date is entered here, if so the charterer will not have to start working the vessel until the exact time mentioned.

Boxes 10 and 11 name the loading and discharging ports and places. Unless a named berth is entered here the owner can select any berth of his choice. This may be quite important in some circumstances. For example if the charterer has his own private berth and stevedore and the owner is responsible for paying stevedoring costs it is likely that the charterer will name his berth. Should he fail to do so the owner would be quite within his rights to demand that the ship is worked at a different berth where stevedoring costs are lower or handling is much quicker. There may be many other reasons why a charterer would wish for the ship to be handled at a specific berth but if this is not recorded here the owner is not obliged to accede to his wishes. From the agents point of view he will need to know how these boxes are completed. He must follow the owners instructions if the charter party does not name a specific berth and he will be obliged to inform the owner if a better berth than that offered by the charterer exists.

Box 12 gives the cargo details. There is also mention of a margin in owners option. Because the stowage factor of a particular type of cargo may vary within certain parameters it is not possible to give the exact quantity in tonnes which will fill the ship. There is usually a margin of between 5 and 10 percent above or below the stated figure. The owner, or more exactly the master, can demand that any figure within this range is delivered to the vessel. In fixture recaps this is usually recorded as say 2500 5% moloo (2500 tonnes, 5 percent more or less owners option.) If the cargo is not of a type which the vessel must load to capacity under stability rules it is sometimes possible for the charterer to be granted a similar option. Should this be so the box will be amended to reflect this.

If the cargo is in bulk the stowage factor should also be recorded here. Occasionally the expected stowage factor will not be achieved and the final cargo may well be outside the margins mentioned. Providing the ship is full the agent can only leave matters to be resolved between the owner and charterer. However if the ship is not full the master may refuse to sail as his ship will be unsafe. Under such circumstances the agent will need to liase with the ship and the charterer until either sufficient cargo is located or some other means of making the ship safe is found. The accepted practice for most bulk cargoes is to put some of the cargo into bags or sacks and to lay these on top of the bulk cargo. This method reduces the natural movement of bulk cargoes experienced when the ship pitches and rolls at sea.

Box 13 and 14 covering freight payment are usually only of interest to the agent if he is entrusted with collection of the freight.

Box 15 indicates to the agent whether the ship's cargo gear may be used.

Box 16 shows the agent the time allowed for working the vessel at his port. Of course if loading is not completed within that period it does not mean that the vessel has to sail part empty. This is just the period of free time allowed to the charterer before he is penalised for delaying the vessel.

Box 17 names the shippers of the cargo. The agent will need to know this in order to present the notice of readiness.

Box 18 details the demurrage rate. Demurrage is the penalty paid by the charterer if the ship takes longer to load or discharge than was agreed. The rate of demurrage is normally given as a fixed sum payable on a daily basis. Fractions of a day will attract a pro-rata penalty.

Box 19 Cancelling date is the date (or time as in box 9) when the charterer may cancel the charter if the vessel has not arrived at the loading port.

Box 20 is of little interest to the agent unless he has been instrumental in negotiating the fixture, in which case he may be due some of the commission in addition to his agency fee.

Box 21 is for additional clauses. There are very few charter parties which are not amended or added to. Additions may be few in number or they may run into dozens of extra clauses covering innumerable eventualities. Additional clauses are sometimes referred to as rider clauses. Some common additions will be discussed following examination of the written clauses below.

Clause 1 says a great deal of interest to the agent. In its unaltered form it makes clear that the vessel is to be always afloat. For many small tidal ports it is quite usual for ships to be loaded at berths which are almost or completely dry at low tide. If the owner agrees to allow his ship to be worked at this type of berth the words 'or safe aground' may be added. This may be re-inforced by adding the abbreviation NAABSA (not always afloat but safe aground) to the port or place in boxes 10 or 11. Regardless of how it is done the owner is only agreeing to let his ship lie safe aground. Should there be any damage to the ship resulting from the lack of water it would be evident that the berth was not safe and the charterer may be held liable for the repairs to the ship. An agent' s expert knowledge of the berths within his port should be made freely available to the owner so as to allow him to determine the suitability of any nominated berth.

The charterer is obliged to load a full and complete cargo, i.e. as much as the ship is permitted to carry in accordance with its documents, regulations and draft limitations.

Clause 1 also makes it plain that although the owner will allow the charterer free use of dunnage and separation material on board the vessel, any additional requirements will have to be provided by the charterer. Should the agent be involved in ordering dunnage etc. he must look to the charterer for payment and not the shipowner.

Finally at the discharge port the owner must deliver the cargo on being paid freight. This part must be read in conjunction with clause 4.

Clause 2 says little of interest to the port agent as it lists the circumstances under which the shipowner accepts responsibility for loss, damages or delays in delivering the cargo.

Clause 3 allows the owner to order the ship to deviate from the normal route under certain circumstances. Although it seems rather loosely worded the owner is not free to take as long as he likes to complete the voyage nor to call at intermediate ports without good reason. Acceptable reasons for deviation would be to land sick seamen, to obtain stores or bunkers, for repairs to the ship, restowing of the cargo if necessary, avoiding war zones and of course for the purposes of saving life or property. Apart from the first few reasons any deviation that does occur is likely to involve an agent in unusual circumstances. The vessel may have deviated for general average purposes, to rescue survivors from an accident or she may even arrive with a salvaged vessel in tow or under tow herself. The agents response to circumstances of this nature are described in a later chapter.

Clause 4 calls for freight to be paid on delivery of the cargo or if required during delivery. Freight payment clauses are one of those most frequently altered from the standard versions. Alternatives to the printed clause here may include freight payable on signing and releasing bills of lading, within a specified time after loading, before breaking bulk, or within a specified time after discharging.

Unless the owner and charterer are well acquainted with each other and come to other commercial arrangements, owners will want to ensure that they have received money before handing over the goods, and charterers wish to retain freight against possible loss or damage to the cargo. One solution is for a large percentage of the freight to be paid before delivery with the balance being paid after the condition and quantity of the cargo has been ascertained.

Where freight is not likely to be paid on signing bills of lading the owner may request the charterer to pay for the port disbursements. The Gencon charter party gives this right automatically for loading port expenses and by negotiation this can be extended also to the discharge port. The percentage surcharge for advance disbursements is also frequently varied or waived.

Clause 5 covering loading costs is one of which the agent must be fully aware. Stevedoring costs can be attributable to either party depending upon which clause is used. No mention is made though of ancillary costs such as lashing, securing or dunnaging or of tallying and surveying. Items of this nature are generally covered by additions to this clause. The agent must give early notice, to stevedores and other contractors, of who is going to pay their charges.

Clause 6 laytime has already been mentioned as the time allowed for the charterer to load or discharge the cargo. In this charter party the preferred way is by allowing a number of hours either for each operation or as a total for both. Both methods are quite normal as is agreeing on a certain tonnage per day. There are still some charterers who insist on agreeing a rate per hatch per day or even worse on the basis of per working hatch per day. Using such methods makes the calculation of laytime extremely complicated.

To calculate laytime used there has to be a starting and finishing point to the operations. Laytime will start to count after the notice of readiness has been tendered. It does not start the moment the NOR is passed to the shipper or charterer as time is allowed for them to arrange labour etc. The general rule is that a NOR presented in the morning office hours will cause laytime to start at the beginning of the afternoon whereas a NOR presented in the afternoon does not cause laytime to start until the next morning.

The Gencon charter party is a little old fashioned in that it considers Saturdays to be working days, this is usually amended so that Saturdays are placed alongside Sundays and holidays.

In Muslim states Fridays are non-working days but Saturdays and Sundays are working days. Holidays of course vary from country to country and sometimes individual ports have local holidays.

Under a Gencon charter no work needs be started until the NOR becomes effective but the time used will count towards laytime as will any time lost waiting for a berth.

Clause 7 concerns itself with demurrage. Demurrage, as we have already said, is a sum of money paid by the charterer to compensate the owner when the vessel takes longer than allowed for loading or discharging.

The rate of demurrage which was agreed may not reflect the true cost to the owner of the delays which may be experienced. In recognition of this fact the time the vessel will be subject to demurrage is limited in the Gencon to 10 days. This does not mean that after the ten days have elapsed the charterer need not pay further penalties. Should such a situation occur the owner will be entitled to take legal action against the charterer for 'damages for detention'. Damages for detention are the same as any other legal damages in that they must be proved by the claimant. In the case of a vessel detained on account of charterers faults, damages would reflect the freight market, costs incurred for berth dues etc. and any other items which the owner can provide evidence of having incurred as a result of the detention.

Finally demurrage is payable day by day. There is a strict principle governing charters that once the allotted time for working has been used and the vessel is on demurrage, no event whatsoever will result in any additional allowances being granted. Although this clause calls for demurrage to be paid day by day, it is more usual for demurrage to be paid when the final sum is calculated. If for any reason the owner feels that the charterer will not pay he can rely on this part of the clause to secure payments as demurrage is incurred.

Clause 8 is the lien clause. A lien is the right to hold some goods, in this case the cargo, as security for payment of sums due. In order to exercise a lien the shipowner will need to retain control of the goods.

Where the payment due has arisen at the loading port and the ship has yet to begin discharging, the owner can exercise his rights by simply refusing to begin discharging.

The list of items for which the owner can expect payment includes 'dead-freight'. Dead-freight occurs when the charterer is unable to provide all the cargo contracted for. The owners calculations would have been based on the contracted figure, and any shortage will have an adverse effect on his income. In order to overcome this effect the charterer is obliged to pay at the agreed freight rate for the difference between the minimum contracted quantity and the actual loading. Unlike true freight no cargo has to be delivered for this money to be deemed earned and it is therefore payable at the outset of the voyage.

The owner would most likely have secured the next employment for his ship and will not wish for the vessel to be unduly delayed. How then can the owner retain control over the goods without them being in the holds of the ship? Firstly the agent should be able to inform the owner of the practices of the chosen discharging berth. Where the berth belongs to the receiver of the cargo it is clear that the shipowner would have no chance to do so. At a public berth the situation is slightly different, by agreeing to pay any storage costs which might be incurred the owner could place the goods ashore and still retain control. The agent must assist the owner by making it clear in writing that the goods must not be released without the shipowner's authority.

When exercising a lien on the goods the owner must ensure their safekeeping and will be responsible for insuring them against loss or destruction. If the exercise of a lien does not achieve the desired result the owner can arrange for the disposal of the goods by sale either by tender or by auction. The agent may well be instrumental in arranging this particularly when his owner principal is based abroad. The proceeds from the sale of the cargo must first be used to pay the storage and other charges, after this the owner may claim his outstanding sums and any balance paid over to the charterer. In the event that selling the goods does not realise enough to pay all the money outstanding the shipowner will still have the right to take legal proceedings against the charterer for the balance.

In some states the legal processes involved in the owner exercising the right to lien are designed more to protect the receiver of the goods than the shipowner. This is more of a risk where the receiver is a state owned or sponsored organisation. There are places in the world where the owner would not be permitted even to retain the cargo in his ship and would be obliged to discharge by legal or more forceful actions. The agents role is clearly to advise the owner of the likely situation in his port.

Clause 9 concerns the signing of bills of lading. In this clause the agent should note that Bills of lading may be signed with a lower freight value than that contracted for. Although any difference is supposed to be paid in cash when the bills are signed, the agent at the discharging port may be unaware of both the true freight due and the amount paid. For this reason it is especially important when an agent is collecting freight for him to check the amount due with the owner.

Clause 10 details what happens when a vessel is unable to arrive at the loading port on or before the date mentioned in box 19. Vessels which are likely to arrive after the cancelling date are a real headache for shipowners. The owner has to request advice from the charterer as to whether or not the charter is to be cancelled. The charterer does not have to declare this immediately, but only 48 hours before the time the owner has told him the vessel will arrive. The voyage time between the vessels present position and the loading port may well be much more than 48 hours but the owner is obliged to begin the voyage and continue until such time as the charterer declares his intention. The agent can assist all parties by keeping them well informed of the vessel's position and passing on communications without delays. It should be noted that only the charterer has the right to cancel the charter.

Clause 11 details what is to happen in case of General average. The concept and problems of General average from the agent's point of view is dealt with in chapter 8.

Clause 12 is of no interest to an agent as it details the limit of damages in cases of non-compliance.

Clause 13 is the agency clause and as such one of the most important from the agent's point of view. The Gencon charter party like so many others calls for the owner to appoint his own agent at both ports. Today's practice whereby charterers reserve the right of selection of the agents leads to many revisions to this clause. The most usual version reads along the lines of "the Owner shall appoint the charterer's nominated agent at both ports". Failure to understand the difference between nomination and appointment often leads to disputes between owners and charterers. However the agent is selected it is clear that his first loyalty is to the party responsible for paying his fees.

Clause 14 covers brokers commissions, where the agent collects freight he may be asked to remit their commissions to the brokers involved. Commissions are usually paid to at least two different brokers. Where the charterer has his own broking department it is usual for an address commission to be paid. An address commission is no different to any other it merely returns to the charterers instead of being paid to an independent broker.

The final three printed clauses cover matters which are normally outside the influence of either the owner or the charterer. Strike, and war clauses could of course come into play at any time anywhere in the world whereas the ice clause is more limited in its application.

Those then are the printed clauses of the Gencon charter party, to these basic clauses are usually added a number of additional or 'rider' clauses. These would cover a whole range of possibilities which for one reason or another either the shipowner or the charterer has insisted be clearly laid down so as to avoid disputes later.

Among the many subjects of rider clauses are substitution of vessels, delays and expenses caused by stowaways and smuggling, additional insurance which might be payable by cargo interests due to the vessels age flag or class, delays from strike action resulting from the crews employment terms and conditions, usage and limitations of ships gear, methods of stowage etc. There are in fact so many possibilities that it is not unusual to have as many as fifty additional rider clauses.

For an agent to see the charter party as a completed document is quite rare. In fact it is not unknown for voyages to be agreed and performed without any document ever being drawn up. This is especially true of the short sea and coastal trades.

When the owners and charterers brokers have completed their negotiations one or other of them will prepare a 'fixture recap'. This is a résumé of the agreed items and by including a reference to the form of charter party used it will be all that is required for either party to understand their rights and responsibilities.

A typical recap might look something like the following:

mv Ruta
blt 1973
2hoha steel sid gless
loa 85 beam 12
2500 dwcc on 5.3m ssw
111500 gr/110000 bale
Malta flag
100 al Lloyds
pandi ocean
h+m 0.8m usd

PORT AGENCY

for:

fcc wheat sf 46
1gsb 1 fr. bay/1gsb 1 arag
lc 2-5 feb
1500 sshinc/36 hrs wp sshex eiu non-rev
NLG 25 pmt intaken fios spout trimmed payable w/i 3 bd s+r
bs/l.
dem NLG 4500 pdpr/fd bends
vsl free exins
chabe
gencon
3.75 ttl.

At first glance this appears to almost unintelligible gobbledygook but as with any specialised subject a little knowledge will soon reveal the message.

The first section describes the ship which will carry the cargo. In this case the ships name is Ruta. Built in 1973 she is a ship with 2 holds and 2 hatches (2hoha), of steel construction. The vessel has a single deck (sid) and is gearless (gless). Her overall length is 85 metres and her beam 12.5. She has a dead weight cargo capacity (dwcc) of 2500 tonnes when loaded to her maximum summer salt water (ssw) draught of 5.3 metres. The grain capacity of the ship is 111500 cubic feet grain and 110000 cubic feet bale. The vessel flies the Maltese flag and is classified with Lloyds Register. She is entered in the Ocean P and I club and has an insured value of US$800,000.

It is interesting to note that the use of cubic feet as a measurement is more popular than cubic metres. Probably because stowage factors are more meaningful and easier to remember when given in cubic feet rather than cubic metres. Wheat with a stowage factor of 46 would be 1.303 if given in cubic metres, Soya meal stowing at 62 would be 1.756 cubic metres clearly the imperial measures are easier to learn.

The second half of the recap contains the essential details of the charter. Namely the vessel is to load a full and complete (fcc) cargo of wheat with a stowage factor of 46 cubic feet per tonne. Loading is to take place at on good safe berth (gsb) at one French port in the Bay of Biscay. Discharging will be again at one good safe berth of one port in the range of Amsterdam, Rotterdam, Antwerp and Ghent. The lay days begin on 2nd Feb and the cancelling date is the 5th Feb. The abbreviation lc may also be noted as lay-can which may be more obvious. This means that the vessel must present herself at the loading port within the dates mentioned. If she is early she may have to wait on her own account until the 2nd but if she arrives later than the 5th she may find the charter cancelled.

The next line covers the loading and discharging rates and conditions. Loading is to take place at the rate of 1500 tonnes per day Saturdays, Sundays and Holidays included (sshinc). Discharging however should be completed in 36 hours weather permitting. Saturdays, Sundays and Holidays are excluded (sshex) even if used (eiu). The time allowed for loading and discharging is not reversible. (For an explanation of Reversible laytime please refer to the section on demurrage and despatch). Then we come to the freight terms which in this case are 25 Netherlands Guilders (NLG) per metric tonne loaded into the ship. Fios is an abbreviation meaning free in, out and stowed. This means that the shipowner does not have to pay any stevedoring charges for loading or discharging the cargo. Spout trimmed refers to the method of trimming (levelling) the cargo. Spout trimming is done by the spout of the loading facility being moved around from the normal position over the centre of the hatch to ensure an even distribution of cargo in the hold rather than a steep sided heap. Freight has to be paid within 3 banking days of signing and releasing bills of lading.

Demurrage (dem) if any is payable at the rate of NLG 4500 per day pro rata (pdpr). The vessel is however free of Despatch (fd) these rates apply at both ends (bends) i.e. the loading and discharging ports.

PORT AGENCY

The vessel is free of extra insurance (ex ins). Additional premiums for cargo insurance are sometimes charged because of the vessels age, flag or class. Some owners will accept these premiums for their own account in order to secure employment for less attractive vessels.

'Chabe' is an abbreviation indicating that the parties have agreed to the appointment of the charterers nominated agent at both ends.

Gencon is the form of the charter party agreed upon and 3.75 ttl is the total percentage of commission that the owner will have to pay to the brokers.

GENERAL CHARTER PARTY FORM

1. Shipbroker	**RECOMMENDED** **THE BALTIC AND INTERNATIONAL MARITIME CONFERENCE** **UNIFORM GENERAL CHARTER (AS REVISED 1922 and 1976)** **INCLUDING "F.I.O." ALTERNATIVE, ETC.** (To be used for trades for which no approved form is in force) **CODE NAME: "GENCON"** Part I
	2. Place and date
3. Owners/Place of business (Cl. 1)	4. Charterers/Place of business (Cl. 1)
5. Vessel's name (Cl. 1)	6. GRT/NRT (Cl. 1)
7. Deadweight cargo carrying capacity in tons (abt.) (Cl. 1)	8. Present position (Cl. 1)
9. Expected ready to load (abt.) (Cl. 1)	
10. Loading port or place (Cl. 1)	11. Discharging port or place (Cl. 1)

12. Cargo (also state quantity and margin in Owners' option, if agreed; if full and complete cargo not agreed state "part cargo") (Cl. 1)

13. Freight rate (also state if payable on delivered or intaken quantity) (Cl. 1)	14. Freight payment (state currency and method of payment; also beneficiary and bank account) (Cl. 4)
15. Loading and discharging costs (state alternative (a) or (b) of Cl. 5; also indicate if vessel is gearless)	16. Laytime (if separate laytime for load. and disch. is agreed, fill in a) and b). If total laytime for load. and disch., fill in c) only) (Cl. 6)
	a) Laytime for loading
17. Shippers (state name and address) (Cl. 6)	b) Laytime for discharging
	c) Total laytime for loading and discharging
18. Demurrage rate (loading and discharging) (Cl. 7)	19. Cancelling date (Cl. 10)

20. Brokerage commission and to whom payable (Cl. 14)

21. Additional clauses covering special provisions, if agreed.

It is mutually agreed that this Contract shall be performed subject to the conditions contained in this Charter which shall include Part I as well as Part II. In the event of a conflict of conditions, the provisions of Part I shall prevail over those of Part II to the extent of such conflict.

Signature (Owners)	Signature (Charterers)

PART II
"Gencon" Charter (As Revised 1922 and 1976)
Including "F.I.O." Alternative, etc.

1. It is agreed between the party mentioned in Box 3 as Owners of the 1
steamer or motor-vessel named in Box 5, of the gross/nett Register 2
tons indicated in Box 6 and carrying about the number of tons of 3
deadweight cargo stated in Box 7, now in position as stated in Box 8 4
and expected ready to load under this Charter about the date in- 5
dicated in Box 9, and the party mentioned as Charterers in Box 4 6
that: 7
The said vessel shall proceed to the loading port or place stated 8
in Box 10 or so near thereto as she may safely get and lie always 9
afloat, and there load a full and complete cargo (if shipment of deck 10
cargo agreed same to be at Charterers' risk) as stated in Box 12 11
(Charterers to provide all mats and/or wood for dunnage and any 12
separations required, the Owners allowing the use of any dunnage 13
wood on board if required) which the Charterers bind themselves to 14
ship, and being so loaded the vessel shall proceed to the discharg- 15
ing port or place stated in Box 11 as ordered on signing Bills of 16
Lading or so near thereto as she may safely get and lie always 17
afloat and there deliver the cargo on being paid freight on delivered 18
or intaken quantity as indicated in Box 13 at the rate stated in 19
Box 13. 20

2. Owners' Responsibility Clause 21
Owners are to be responsible for loss of or damage to the goods 22
or for delay in delivery of the goods only in case the loss, damage 23
or delay has been caused by the improper or negligent stowage of 24
the goods (unless stowage performed by shippers/Charterers or their 25
stevedores or servants) or by personal want of due diligence on the 26
part of the Owners or their Manager to make the vessel in all respects 27
seaworthy and to secure that she is properly manned, equipped and 28
supplied or by the personal act or default of the Owners or their 29
Manager. 30
And the Owners are responsible for no loss or damage or delay 31
arising from any other cause whatsoever, even from the neglect or 32
default of the Captain or crew or some other person employed by the 33
Owners on board or ashore for whose acts they would, but for this 34
clause, be responsible, or from unseaworthiness of the vessel on 35
loading or commencement of the voyage or at any time whatsoever. 36
Damage caused by contact with or leakage, smell or evaporation 37
from other goods or by the inflammable or explosive nature or in- 38
sufficient package of other goods not to be considered as caused 39
by improper or negligent stowage, even if in fact so caused. 40

3. Deviation Clause 41
The vessel has liberty to call at any port or ports in any order, for 42
any purpose, to sail without pilots, to tow and or assist vessels in 43
all situations, and also to deviate for the purpose of saving life and 44
or property. 45

4. Payment of Freight 46
The freight to be paid in the manner prescribed in Box 14 in cash 47
without discount on delivery of the cargo at mean rate of exchange 48
ruling on day or days of payment, the receivers of the cargo being 49
bound to pay freight on account during delivery, if required by Cap- 50
tain or Owners. 51
Cash for vessel's ordinary disbursements at port of loading to be 52
advanced by Charterers if required at highest current rate of ex- 53
change, subject to two per cent. to cover insurance and other ex- 54
penses. 55

5. Loading/Discharging Costs 56
* *(a) Gross Terms* 57
The cargo to be brought alongside in such a manner as to enable 58
vessel to take the goods with her own tackle. Charterers to procure 59
and pay the necessary men on shore or on board the lighters to do 60
the work there, vessel only having the cargo on board. 61
If the loading takes place by elevator, cargo to be put free in vessel's 62
holds. Owners only paying trimming expenses. 63
Any pieces and or packages of cargo over two tons weight, shall be 64
loaded, stowed and discharged by Charterers at their risk and expense. 65
The cargo to be received by Merchants at their risk and expense 66
alongside the vessel not beyond the reach of her tackle. 67
* *(b) F.i.o. and free stowed/trimmed* 68
The cargo shall be brought into the holds. loaded. stowed and or trim- 69
med and taken from the holds and discharged by the Charterers or 70
their Agents, free of any risk, liability and expense whatsoever to the 71
Owners. 72
The Owners shall provide winches. motive power and winchmen from 73
the Crew if requested and permitted; if not, the Charterers shall 74
provide and pay for winchmen from shore and or cranes, if any. (This 75
provision shall not apply if vessel is gearless and stated as such in 76
Box 15). 77
* *indicate alternative (a) or (b), as agreed, in Box 15* 78

6. Laytime 79
* *(a) Separate laytime for loading and discharging* 80
The cargo shall be loaded within the number of running hours as 81
indicated in Box 16, weather permitting, Sundays and holidays ex- 82
cepted, unless used, in which event time actually used shall count. 83
The cargo shall be discharged within the number of running hours 84
as indicated in Box 16, weather permitting, Sundays and holidays ex- 85
cepted, unless used, in which event time actually used shall count. 86
* *(b) Total laytime for loading and discharging* 87
The cargo shall be loaded and discharged within the number of total 88
running hours as indicated in Box 16, weather permitting, Sundays and 89
holidays excepted. unless used, in which event time actually used 90
shall count. 91
(c) Commencement of laytime (loading and discharging) 92
Laytime for loading and discharging shall commence at 1 p.m. if 93
notice of readiness is given before noon, and at 6 a.m. next working 94
day if notice given during office hours after noon. Notice at loading 95
port to be given to the Shippers named in Box 17. 96
Time actually used before commencement of laytime shall count. 97
Time lost in waiting for berth to count as loading or discharging 98
time. as the case may be. 99
* *indicate alternative (a) or (b) as agreed, in Box 16.* 100

7. Demurrage 101
Ten running days on demurrage at the rate stated in Box 18 per 102
day or pro rata for any part of a day, payable day by day, to be 103
allowed Merchants altogether at ports of loading and discharging. 104

8. Lien Clause 105
Owners shall have a lien on the cargo for freight, dead-freight, 106
demurrage and damages for detention. Charterers shall remain re- 107
sponsible for dead-freight and demurrage (including damages for 108
detention), incurred at port of loading. Charterers shall also remain 109
responsible for freight and demurrage (including damages for deten- 110
tion) incurred at port of discharge, but only to such extent as the 111
Owners have been unable to obtain payment thereof by exercising 112
the lien on the cargo. 113

9. Bills of Lading 114
The Captain to sign Bills of Lading at such rate of freight as 115
presented without prejudice to this Charterparty, but should the 116
freight by Bills of Lading amount to less than the total chartered 117
freight the difference to be paid to the Captain in cash on signing 118
Bills of Lading. 119

10. Cancelling Clause 120
Should the vessel not be ready to load (whether in berth or not) on 121
or before the date indicated in Box 19, Charterers have the option 122
of cancelling this contract, such option to be declared, if demanded, 123
at least 48 hours before vessel's expected arrival at port of loading. 124
Should the vessel be delayed on account of average or otherwise, 125
Charterers to be informed as soon as possible, and if the vessel is 126
delayed for more than 10 days after the day she is stated to be 127
expected ready to load, Charterers have the option of cancelling this 128
contract, unless a cancelling date has been agreed upon. 129

11. General Average 130
General average to be settled according to York-Antwerp Rules, 131
1974. Proprietors of cargo to pay the cargo's share in the general 132
expenses even if same have been necessitated through neglect or 133
default of the Owners' servants (see clause 2). 134

12. Indemnity 135
Indemnity for non-performance of this Charterparty, proved damages, 136
not exceeding estimated amount of freight. 137

13. Agency 138
In every case the Owners shall appoint his own Broker or Agent both 139
at the port of loading and the port of discharge. 140

14. Brokerage 141
A brokerage commission at the rate stated in Box 20 on the freight 142
earned is due to the party mentioned in Box 20. 143
In case of non-execution at least ⅓ of the brokerage on the estimated 144
amount of freight and dead-freight to be paid by the Owners to the 145
Brokers as indemnity for the latter's expenses and work. In case of 146
more voyages the amount of indemnity to be mutually agreed. 147

15. GENERAL STRIKE CLAUSE 148
Neither Charterers nor Owners shall be responsible for the con- 149
sequences of any strikes or lock-outs preventing or delaying the 150
fulfilment of any obligations under this contract. 151
If there is a strike or lock-out affecting the loading of the cargo, 152
or any part of it, when vessel is ready to proceed from her last port 153
or at any time during the voyage to the port or ports of loading or 154
after her arrival there, Captain or Owners may ask Charterers to 155
declare, that they agree to reckon the laydays as if there were no 156
strike or lock-out. Unless Charterers have given such declaration in 157
writing (by telegram, if necessary) within 24 hours, Owners shall 158
have the option of cancelling this contract. If part cargo has already 159
been loaded, Owners must proceed with same, (freight payable on 160
loaded quantity only) having liberty to complete with other cargo 161
on the way for their own account. 162
If there is a strike or lock-out affecting the discharge of the cargo 163
on or after vessel's arrival at or off port of discharge and same has 164
not been settled within 48 hours, Receivers shall have the option of 165
keeping vessel waiting until such strike or lock-out is at an end 166
against paying half demurrage after expiration of the time provided 167
for discharging, or of ordering the vessel to a safe port where she 168
can safely discharge without risk of being detained by strike or lock- 169
out. Such orders to be given within 48 hours after Captain or Owners 170
have given notice to Charterers of the strike or lock-out affecting 171
the discharge. On delivery of the cargo at such port, all conditions 172
of this Charterparty and of the Bill of Lading shall apply and vessel 173
shall receive the same freight as if she had discharged at the 174
original port of destination, except that if the distance of the sub- 175
stituted port exceeds 100 nautical miles, the freight on the cargo 176
delivered at the substituted port to be increased in proportion. 177

16. War Risks ("Voywar 1950") 178
(1) In these clauses "War Risks" shall include any blockade or any 179
action which is announced as a blockade by any Government or by any 180
belligerent or by any organized body, sabotage, piracy, and any actual 181
or threatened war, hostilities, warlike operations, civil war, civil com- 182
motion, or revolution. 183
(2) If at any time before the Vessel commences loading, it appears that 184
performance of the contract will subject the Vessel or her Master and 185
crew or her cargo to war risks at any stage of the adventure, the Owners 186
shall be entitled by letter or telegram despatched to the Charterers, to 187
cancel this Charter. 188
(3) The Master shall not be required to load cargo or to continue 189
loading or to proceed on or to sign Bill(s) of Lading for any adventure 190
on which or any port at which it appears that the Vessel, her Master 191
and crew or her cargo will be subjected to war risks. In the event of 192
the exercise by the Master of his right under this Clause after port or 193
full cargo has been loaded, the Master shall be at liberty either to 194
discharge such cargo at the loading port or to proceed therewith. 195
In the latter case the Vessel shall have liberty to carry other cargo 196
for Owners' benefit and accordingly to proceed to and load or 197
discharge such other cargo at any other port or ports whatsoever, 198
backwards or forwards, although in a contrary direction to or out of or 199
beyond the ordinary route. In the event of the Master electing to 200
proceed with part cargo under this Clause freight shall in any case 201
be payable on the quantity delivered. 202
(4) If at the time the Master elects to proceed with part or full cargo 203
under Clause 3, or after the Vessel has left the loading port, or the 204

PART II
"Gencon" Charter (As Revised 1922 and 1976)
Including "F.I.O." Alternative, etc.

last of the loading ports, if more than one, it appears that further 205
performance of the contract will subject the Vessel, her Master and 206
crew or her cargo, to war risks, the cargo shall be discharged, or if 207
the discharge has been commenced shall be completed, at any safe 208
port in vicinity of the port of discharge as may be ordered by the 209
Charterers. If no such orders shall be received from the Charterers 210
within 48 hours after the Owners have despatched a request by 211
telegram to the Charterers for the nomination of a substitute discharg- 212
ing port, the Owners shall be at liberty to discharge the cargo at 213
any safe port which they may, in their discretion, decide on and such 214
discharge shall be deemed to be due fulfilment of the contract of 215
affreightment. In the event of cargo being discharged at any such 216
other port, the Owners shall be entitled to freight as if the discharge 217
had been effected at the port or ports named in the Bill(s) of Lading 218
or to which the Vessel may have been ordered pursuant thereto. 219

(5) (a) The Vessel shall have liberty to comply with any directions 220
or recommendations as to loading, departure, arrival, routes, ports 221
of call, stoppages, destination, zones, waters, discharge, delivery or 222
in any other wise whatsoever (including any direction or recom- 223
mendation not to go to the port of destination or to delay proceeding 224
thereto or to proceed to some other port) given by any Government or 225
by any belligerent or by any organized body engaged in civil war, 226
hostilities or warlike operations or by any person or body acting or 227
purporting to act as or with the authority of any Government or 228
belligerent or of any such organized body or by any committee or 229
person having under the terms of the war risks insurance on the 230
Vessel, the right to give any such directions or recommendations. If, 231
by reason of or in compliance with any such direction or recom- 232
mendation, anything is done or is not done, such shall not be deemed 233
a deviation. 234

(b) If, by reason of or in compliance with any such directions or re- 235
commendations, the Vessel does not proceed to the port or ports 236
named in the Bill(s) of Lading or to which she may have been 237
ordered pursuant thereto, the Vessel may proceed to any port as 238
directed or recommended or to any safe port which the Owners in 239
their discretion may decide on and there discharge the cargo. Such 240
discharge shall be deemed to be due fulfilment of the contract of 241
affreightment and the Owners shall be entitled to freight as if 242
discharge had been effected at the port or ports named in the Bill(s) 243
of Lading or to which the Vessel may have been ordered pursuant 244
thereto. 245

(6) All extra expenses (including insurance costs) involved in discharg- 246
ing cargo at the loading port or in reaching or discharging the cargo 247
at any port as provided in Clauses 4 and 5 (b) hereof shall be paid 248
by the Charterers and/or cargo owners, and the Owners shall have 249
a lien on the cargo for all moneys due under these Clauses. 250

17. GENERAL ICE CLAUSE 251
Port of loading 252
(a) In the event of the loading port being inaccessible by reason of 253
ice when vessel is ready to proceed from her last port or at any 254
time during the voyage or on vessel's arrival or in case frost sets in 255
after vessel's arrival, the Captain for fear of being frozen in is at 256
liberty to leave without cargo, and this Charter shall be null and 257
void. 258

(b) If during loading the Captain, for fear of vessel being frozen in, 259
deems it advisable to leave, he has liberty to do so with what cargo 260
he has on board and to proceed to any other port or ports with 261
option of completing cargo for Owners' benefit for any port or ports 262
including port of discharge. Any part cargo thus loaded under this 263
Charter to be forwarded to destination at vessel's expense but 264
against payment of freight, provided that no extra expenses be 265
thereby caused to the Receivers, freight being paid on quantity 266
delivered (in proportion if lumpsum), all other conditions as per 267
Charter. 268

(c) In case of more than one loading port, and if one or more of 269
the ports are closed by ice, the Captain or Owners to be at liberty 270
either to load the part cargo at the open port and fill up elsewhere 271
for their own account or to declare the Charter null and void unless Charterers agree to load full cargo at the open 273
port. 274

(d) This Ice Clause not to apply in the Spring. 275

Port of discharge 276

(a) Should ice (except in the Spring) prevent vessel from reaching 277
port of discharge Receivers shall have the option of keeping vessel 278
waiting until the re-opening of navigation and paying demurrage, or 279
of ordering the vessel to a safe and immediately accessible port 280
where she can safely discharge without risk of detention by ice. 281
Such orders to be given within 48 hours after Captain or Owners 282
have given notice to Charterers of the impossibility of reaching port 283
of destination. 284

(b) If during discharging the Captain for fear of vessel being frozen 285
in deems it advisable to leave, he has liberty to do so with what 286
cargo he has on board and to proceed to the nearest accessible 287
port where she can safely discharge. 288

(c) On delivery of the cargo at such port, all conditions of the Bill 289
of Lading shall apply and vessel shall receive the same freight as 290
if she had discharged at the original port of destination, except that if 291
the distance of the substituted port exceeds 100 nautical miles, the 292
freight on the cargo delivered at the substituted port to be increased 293
in proportion. 294

Printed and sold by Witherby & Company Limited, 32/36 Aylesbury Street, London EC1R 0ET.   Tel. No. 071 251 5341   Fax No. 071 251 1296
by authority of The Baltic and International Maritime Council, (BIMCO) Copenhagen.

Contracts of Affreightment

A voyage charter party usually covers a single cargo, there are occasions when both the owner and the charterer agree to a specialised contract of affreightment (CoA) which will cover several voyages by one or more vessels. A CoA may be agreed for a specific volume of cargo to be moved at agreed intervals until the whole quantity has been shipped or it may be agreed for a fixed period or number of voyages during which time as much cargo as possible is shipped. Whichever method is chosen the basic terms will usually refer either to a specific form of charter party or will be specially drawn up incorporating elements from several different standard forms.

Laytime, Demurrage and Despatch

Demurrage and despatch are two sides of the same coin. Demurrage is provided for in all but the most obscure voyage charter parties. It is the penalty payable by the charterer for being unable to load or discharge the vessel in the agreed time. Despatch is, by contrast, paid by the owner to the charterer when the vessel completes operations inside the time allowed. Despatch will only appear in charter parties if it is specifically agreed upon and is customarily fixed at half the demurrage rate. Demurrage and despatch calculations are quite simple in that one only has to multiply the time lost or saved by the appropriate rate. Calculating the time is however much more complicated.

We have seen that vessels working under voyage charter parties have an agreed timescale in which to complete loading and/or discharging operations. Because of the differing interpretations which have at one time or another been placed upon commonly used terms and phrases a standard interpretation was considered desirable. BIMCO responded to this by publishing the 'Voylay' rules in collaboration with other international shipping organisations. The Voylay rules are a good reference point but are only considered as definitive if they are expressly incorporated into a charter party.

104

Laytime is the time allowed for loading or discharging of the vessel. The commencement of laytime is dependent on the relevant charter party clause and the timely deliverance of the NOR. In order to present the NOR on time the agent will need to know at what point it may be presented. There is probably no more controversial point in tramp shipping than when a ship is considered to have as arrived. From the charterer's view the later the better and from the owner's side the reverse is true. Certainly a ship cannot begin working until it has physically reached the berth intended for that purpose, but there should be nothing to prevent the charterer from making preparations so that the ship commences working immediately.

From our brief look at the Gencon charter party we saw that time will begin counting at the commencement of the next working period after the notice is given. What is not stated is where the ship must be before NOR is able to be presented. It does state that any time lost in waiting for a berth is to count as laytime. From this we can deduce that the NOR should be given when the ship is on the berth, unless for reasons of congestion she is prevented from berthing immediately. Other charter parties may be much more specific and say that NOR can be tendered in accordance with one or more of the following terms:-

'whether in port or not' (WIPON), 'whether in berth or not' (WIBON), 'whether in free practique or not' (WIFPON) or 'whether in customs clearance or not (WICCON) in fixture recaps the full combination of these is sometimes further abbreviated and appears as 'NOR may be tendered wwww'. Use of these terms will allow the shipowner to give notice as soon as he approaches the port. This can make a great deal of difference where the passage time from pilot station to berth means that the ship arrives at the berth in a later working period than that when it arrived at the pilot station. Using the times from the Gencon the laytime could conceivably start 17 hours earlier (from 1300 instead of 0600 the next day).

Some charter parties recognise the fact that the passage to the berth is an unavoidable loss of time and will include a provision that 'time used in moving to berth not to count'. This phrase does not alter the fact that time can begin to count before the vessel is actually berthed. It merely allows the passage time to be deducted from the laytime used always assuming that the vessel has not been so long delayed at anchor that demurrage has already begun to accrue.

Given the endless permutations of possibilities the golden rule for all agents must be to tender notice of readiness as soon as the vessel arrives at anchor or at the pilot station. The charterer will soon reject the notice if it has been given too early. To protect the owner's position the agent should not cancel earlier notices but should refer to them and advise the updated position.

Once laytime has started the next task is to calculate how much is allowed. The most simple method is to allow a fixed total number of days or hours for the cargo to be worked. Using this method time will begin counting in accordance with the terms of the charter party and will continue until the cargo is loaded. This time is deducted from the total allowed with the balance being left for the discharging which will again commence in accordance with the charter party terms. When all the time allowed is used up in the loading of the cargo the vessel will come on demurrage until loading is completed and as soon as the vessel arrives at the discharge port demurrage will begin to accrue regardless of the notice period.

This simplest method can be amended so that a separate time is allowed for loading and discharging. Where separate times are allowed there must be two calculations one for the loading port and one for the discharge port. The result may be that demurrage is payable on one and despatch on the other. When separate times for loading and discharging are agreed charterers sometimes insist on 'reversible' laytime. This has the effect of allowing time lost at the loading end to be offset against time saved at the discharging port. Of course the loading calculations can be made quite early but if the charterer insists on reversible laytime the owner must wait until discharging is completed before knowing what sums are due. Reversible and total laytime effectively remove the owners right of lien for demurrage at the loading port since no calculations can be made.

Instead of a fixed time period for each operation the parties may agree upon a daily tonnage rate. To calculate the time here it is necessary to divide the tonnage loaded by the agreed rate. The rate may be different at the loading and discharging ports. It is not uncommon to use a tonnage rate for one port and a time period for the discharging port.

All the variations so far described have assumed a day to be a period of 24 hours commencing from the moment the NOR has been accepted. No mention has been made either of weekends and holidays.

Taking first the question of weekends these may be specifically excluded or included by agreement. In the fixture recap above we discussed the implications of the terms SSHINC and SSHEX and how in some countries Fridays, and not Sundays, are holidays. More modern charter parties take into account the reluctance of labour to work late before weekends. There is a regularly used clause which reads 'Time from 1700 hrs. Friday, or days preceding holidays, until 0800 hrs. Monday, or days following a holiday not to count'. Once a vessel has come on demurrage weekends lose their significance and become days like any other.

The 24 hour day is also qualified in most cases. The easiest qualification to work with is 'w.p.' or weather permitting. In this event any actual working time lost up to the completion of the operation or until the vessel comes onto demurrage is simply deducted from the time used. There is another frequently used qualification which has more profound effects on calculations, 'WWD' or weather working day is quite different from weather permitting. This qualification allows the charterer to deduct from laytime any period of weather which would have caused the vessel to stop working regardless of the fact that no working was actually taking place at the time. The agent must now record all periods of bad weather, day and night, as well as during any time the vessel was waiting at anchor.

So far all the terms mentioned have referred to the time for the ship as a whole. There are a few trades where it is customary to allow a rate per hatch per day. On a ship with several hatches of different sizes this can make calculations almost impossible. The logical solution is to consider that the largest hold will invariably take the longest to work and to base the maximum time on this hold. Ships holds may have more than one hatch and where this is the case the accepted method is to take the cargo tonnage of the largest hold, divide it by the daily rate in the charter party and divide that figure by the number of hatches serving the hold. The final result is the time allowed for the whole ship to complete.

Given the problems and legal rulings on laytime it is surprising that some owners and charterers still make life difficult by insisting on obscure out-moded methods of describing the time allowed. Terms such as 'fast as can custom of port' (faccop) and 'customary quick despatch' (cqd) are still to be found in some fixtures. One can only hope that the parties are able to reach an amicable agreement on demurrage and despatch, given such imprecise terms to work with.

Demurrage and despatch are calculated from a laytime statement similar to that reproduced below. Agents are not often called upon today to calculate demurrage but they may be asked to collect sums due from charterers. Owners who make extensive use of modern technology may have computer software programmes which calculate laytime once essential voyage data has been keyed in.

Laytime Statement

m.v. _____ **Loading/Discharging at** _____

Charterers _____ **C/P dated** _____

Tonnage _____ **C/P Rate** _____ **Time allowed** _____

Demurrage Rate _____ **Despatch Rate** _____

Day	Date	Time		Remarks	Laytime Used			Time saved/ on demurrage		
		from	to		D	H	M	D	H	M
			Total Time used.							
			Time on demurrage							

Despatch/Demurrage: _____ **days @** _____ **per day =** _____

Dated _____

PORT AGENCY

Chapter Six

THE AGENT AND DOCUMENTS

Introduction

In earlier chapters the forms required for customs purposes were discussed and references made to manifests and time sheets or statement of facts. There are a number of other documents of varying degrees of importance which will pass across an agents desk in the course of his duties. Some of them may need to be prepared or completed by the agent himself. Others will merely have to be passed on to the correct parties.

Liner vessels and tramp vessels will have differing documentary requirements reflecting their differing trades. There will however be some documents common to both types of vessels. Similarly tankers will have some unique requirements not required for dry cargo ships.

Before considering documents for use by third parties it is perhaps worthwhile mentioning that probably, to the agent at least, the most helpful document is his own checklist.

Agents practices in this regard vary with many individuals relying on their memory rather than using prepared lists to ensure relevant questions about matters such as bunker figures, fresh water requirements, and operational matters are asked at the right time and action taken as necessary. Certainly experience makes much of the work second nature but mistakes can always be made and it is better to have something to which others can refer whenever necessary. This is of especial importance on large agency offices where different people may take over the handling of a ship.

Returning to the third party documents which agents will encounter and their uses it is useful to divide them into two groups. Those which relate to the ship and those relating to the cargo.

Ships Documents

Notice of Readiness. (NOR)

This document is not used for vessels operating in liner trades but will be required for both tankers and dry cargo vessels operating under charter parties.

The NOR is an extremely important document which notifies the charters of a ship of its readiness to load or discharge cargo. The tendering of an NOR is the start of the process whereby laytime allowed under the charter party begins to count. Charter Parties usually contain explicit details of when and how an NOR can be tendered.

An NOR may be a pre-printed or standard form or merely a written note. An example of typical wording is given on the following page.

NOTICE OF READINESS. To whom it may concern. Please be advised that M.V.......................has arrived at ....(port or place) ....on ....(date)...... at.... (time)...... and is in all respects ready to load/discharge a cargo of... under Charter Party dated...................................Laytime to count in accordance with relevant terms and conditions of said Charter Party.

Tendered at ....(time)......... on............date).........by..........(owner master agent)...

Notice accepted at ....(time).......... on ....(date)............ by ....(charterer)...........

Time to count from...

Tanker charter parties commonly allow the notice of readiness to be given on arrival at the pilot station or anchorage with time beginning to count six hours after arrival at any time day or night. This is a reflection of the fact that oil terminals operate around the clock.

The proper time for tendering notice of readiness by dry cargo vessels has no such commonality amongst different charter party forms. Exactly where a vessel must be to be considered ready has always been a contentious point between owners and charters.

Charters will argue that a vessel cannot be ready unless she is at the working berth. On the other hand owners will argue that the vessel may be ready even if she cannot berth due to congestion or tidal conditions. Owners have also discovered that some ports are remarkably slow in granting customs clearance or official approval to proceed and work in a port (free practique).

The time of readiness of vessels which for whatever reason cannot berth immediately may be further complicated if the anchorage or waiting place is outside the port limits. The charters argument here is that the vessel cannot be ready if it has not even arrived at the port.

PORT AGENCY

Whatever the rights and wrongs of each argument it is an undeniable fact that despite numerous legal cases the question of what is an arrived ship is still one which cannot be answered with any certainty. In an attempt to resolve this ambiguity charter party clauses contain terms such as NOR may be tendered..... 'whether in berth or not' (WIBON) 'whether in port or not (WIPON) 'whether in free practique or not' (WIFPON).

Aside from where the vessel must be, the proper time for tendering notice of readiness must also be taken into account, Dry cargo vessels normally have to tender notice within office hours. This term has also lead to problems since 'office hours' is a very loose wording. The modern trend is to call for notice to be tendered between certain defined hours in normal working days. It is common for this time to begin counting at 1300 or 1400 hours if the NOR is tendered before noon or at 0800 hours if tendered after noon.

In cases where the notice has to be tendered when the vessel has berthed it is normal practice for the agent to receive the notice from the master and to pass it on to the correct party without delay. This is particularly important when berthing takes place shortly before noon or near to the end of the working day as detailed in the charter party. Failure to do this will result in laytime beginning later. There is no excuse for most agents to delay in sending NORS. The efficient agent will prepare an NOR to be sent automatically by telex or fax to coincide with the expected berthing of the vessel. In the event that the NOR is sent but the vessel fails to berth no damage is done and the NOR must merely be sent again at a later time.

Where the charter party allows for the NOR to be tendered with the vessel at anchor or outside the port, the agent needs to monitor the vessels position, obtain official confirmation if necessary from pilots or harbour masters and to tender the NOR on behalf of the owners. Once again due regard must be given to timing.

The biggest danger for the agent is failing to read and interpret the charter party correctly.

This is best illustrated by the example of a vessel which is allowed 2 1/2 days to discharge a cargo. The charter party terms allowed NOR to be tendered within the hours of 0900 - 1700 on normal working days WIBON, WIPON. The vessel arrived at anchor at 1000 hrs on a Wednesday but due to congestion did not berth until the following Tuesday at 0800 hrs. The agent believing that the NOR could only be tendered after arrival at the berth tendered notice at 0900 on the Tuesday the vessel berthed. Time began counting at 1400 that day and the vessel completed at 1700 on the next day. The time used was therefore 1 1/2 days resulting in one days despatch being due to the charterer.

Had the agent delivered notice at 1000 on the Wednesday as allowed by the charter party. Time would have began counting at 1400 on Wednesday and would have expired at 1700 on Friday, as the vessel did not complete until 1700 the following Wednesday the charterer would have had to pay 5 days demurrage.

In the case in question the demurrage rate had been fixed at US$ 2000 per day with despatch at half this. The nett loss to the owner, who should have received US$ 10000 in demurrage but who ended up paying despatch of US$ 1500, was US$ 8500, overall a very costly mistake by the agent.

After tendering the notice of readiness the agent will be attending to the official requirements of the vessel. to do this he will need to complete customs declarations and immigration forms. When reporting or clearing ships the agent will need to produce the various ships documents. Again these do vary from country to country but are based on standard formats.

Details of these forms and their function appeared in Chapter 3.

PORT AGENCY

Statement of Facts and Time Sheets

The record of arrival times, working periods and interruptions is known as the 'statement of facts'. Although there are standard forms many agents prefer to use their own documents. The amount of information given will vary but it is better to include information than to omit it. Extraneous facts can be disregarded but missing records may take hours or days of investigating. The statement of facts is the basic document from which the time sheet is prepared. The statement of facts records all that happens during the call, the time sheet is used to calculate the demurage due or payable, again there are proprietary forms but agents often design their own. When completing these documents it is important that the charter party terms have been understood and required information included. Unless the agent knows exactly the terms of the charter party he should include sufficient information to cover all eventualities. Remembering for example that 'wwd' terms will necessitate including weather details for every hour of the day and night.

Cargo Documents

Bill of Lading

First and foremost of the cargo documents is the bill of lading. This document is fundamental to shipping and has been and will continue to be the subject of legislation and argument.

The bill of lading is a multi-purpose document which fulfills three functions.

The first function is as a receipt for goods. As the cargo is brought into the ship the cargo mate will prepare a 'mate's receipt' this will contain details of the number and type of goods and their condition. From this 'mate's receipt' the details needed for the bill of lading are extracted. Entered onto a bill of lading form they are presented to the master for signature. The master's signature is an admission that the cargo is on board and in the ship's care. The agent may well be the person who is to prepare

116

bills of lading, this is almost certainly true of liner ships but in the case of tramp ships it is not unusual for the charterer or shipper to prepare the bills of lading. He may even be given permission to sign them on behalf of the ship providing the information on the bill does not conflict with the mate's receipt.

Bills of lading are not usually issued as single documents although there is no reason why they should not be. The usual practice is to issue sets of bills containing three originals and any number of copies. The master is required to sign all three original bills and to hand them back to the shipper. The shipper will distribute the bills as necessary.

As a receipt for goods it is important that the bill of lading contains a true description of the goods and their condition on loading. Where the cargo differs in any way from its basic description the master will wish to protect himself and the owner by entering on the front of the bill a remark concerning the quality or quantity of the cargo. Bills which are qualified are said to be 'marked' or 'dirty' bills. A bill without any remarks is known as a 'clean' bill. There are certain commodities which frequently appear to be in a poor condition but which are actually quite normal. One such commodity is steel. Steel is very prone to atmospheric rust, a light coating which appears under all but the most perfect conditions. A light coating of rust may well be of little concern to the buyer and seller but the master would almost certainly want to see the condition recorded on the bill of lading. Should he fail to do this the cargo owner might claim that the rust was due to leaking hatches or inadequate ventilation and make a claim against the shipowner.

A bill of lading which is dirty is certain to cause some problems in its second role as a negotiable document. The cargo which is loaded onto a ship may well be sold during the voyage from loading to discharging port. Some cargoes may change hands several times even on short voyages. This is particularly true in the case of oil cargoes, one of which actually changed hands over forty times between Novorossiisk in Russia and the U.K.

117

PORT AGENCY

When cargoes which are on the high seas are sold it is patently obvious that the goods themselves cannot be moved between seller and buyer. The bill of lading is the document which is passed between the parties. Each time a bill of lading is passed on the seller endorses the back of the bill.

Where the bill is dirty the buyer may not be prepared to continue with the purchase since the true condition of the goods may be different from that being proclaimed by the seller.

Further difficulties arise when the bill is used for letter of credit purposes. A letter of credit is a special arrangement made by banks for assisting and financing international trade.

The buyer of goods will deposit the purchase price with a bank, or the bank may loan him the money for the purchase. When the seller is able to produce a signed original bill of lading to the bank the money for the goods is handed over to him and the bill retained by the bank or passed onto the buyer. The banks are very reluctant to hand over money when the bill which is presented to them is dirty.

To overcome this situation the charterer commonly asks for the shipowner to allow the issue of clean bills of lading and offers a 'letter of indemnity'. A letter of indemnity, sometimes referred to as an LoI, is a document in which the charterer promises to cover any costs incurred by the owner as a result of signing clean bills when 'marked' bills should have been issued. Letters of indemnity of potentially fraudulent documents because future endorsees are not aware of the true cargo condition.

Because they are fraudulent and could be used to deceive an innocent third party, no court of law will uphold an owners claim against the issuer of an LoI.

Shipowners do still accept letters of indemnity either because they know the parties concerned and their usual practices, or as a commercial risk. An agent entrusted with issuing bills of lading should never accept an offered letter of indemnity without the express written authority of the shipowner.

In order to collect the cargo at the discharging port it will be necessary for the party claiming it to present an original bill of lading to the port agent. It should be remembered that there are more than one originals of each bill. The agent is normally obliged to deliver the goods to the first party to present an original bill. There are exceptions to this rule, for example where an original has been lost or stolen.

Despite their obvious value bills of lading are sometimes carelessly treated and misplaced. When this happens the cargo owner has to make some alternate arrangement to obtain possession of his cargo. He may be able to convince the shipowner of his entitlement and take the delivery of the cargo against the shipowner's instruction to the agent to release. This is not a very likely scenario and more often than not the shipowner will be looking for some form of protection against future claims should it transpire that the person claiming the goods was not entitled to receive them. The most common form of such protection is again a letter of indemnity. In this case the letter of indemnity should bind the issuer to indemnify the shipowner against any possible claims as well as promising to present the original bills should they eventually be discovered. There are very few shipowners who will accept this indemnity unless it has been countersigned by a first class bank. The countersigning by the bank is an added safeguard because the bank will need to set aside some of the cargo owner's funds for a period of several years in case an action is commenced under the indemnity. The length of time will depend on the law of the country or the contract which may vary substantially. The presentation of a Letter of Indemnity to the shipowner may be done through the port agent who should make sure that he verifies the countersigning by the bank to be valid.

Should the agent ever have suspicions about the right of the person to possess the bill of lading he should make urgent enquiries before allowing the delivery of any goods.

The final role of the bill of lading is as evidence of a contract. We have seen that in tramp shipping the contract between the shipowner and the charterer is the charter party. A bill of lading for cargoes carried under charter parties is a relatively simple document. The front of the bill will carry the details of the goods and the masters signature. The reverse will have a few printed clauses. The first clause is a statement that the goods were shipped under a charter party, the terms and conditions of which are the contract of carriage. The second clause will be a 'clause paramount'. The clause paramount which also appears in some charter parties has the effect of making the contract subject to one or other versions of the Hague or Hague-Visby rules.

These rules are internationally agreed and adopted conventions covering the rights and responsibilities of parties to a contract for the carriage of goods. In instances where the bill of lading has been transferred to a third party the conditions of carriage will move away from the charter party terms and the contract will become covered by the declared version of the Hague rules.

If the shipowner wishes to preserve any of the special agreed provisions of the charter party he will have to agree with the charterer that the relevant clauses are added to the bill of lading. Some owners have their own forms of tramp bills of lading but the most commonly used is the BIMCO 'Congen' Bill.

Liner bills of lading are superficially similar to charter party bills but the reverse contains far more clauses. Because the shipper and the ship owner have not negotiated the terms of carriage the shipper is obliged to accept the owners own terms . The terms and therefore the contract of carriage itself are fully contained in the bill of lading.

The bill of lading will contain information as to when freight is payable and sometimes the amount of freight. When the freight is paid at the load port before sailing they will be marked 'freight paid' or 'freight prepaid'. It is not uncommon for the contract to call for freight to be prepaid but for money not to have been received by the owner before sailing. When this happens the owner will instruct the agent to refrain from handing over the bills until freight has actually been received.

Freight which is payable at destination will be marked with that wording or 'freight collect'. An agent presented with bills thus marked should not release the goods until he has ascertained that freight has indeed been paid. Occasionally freight will be payable at some other place or time and this will be recorded upon the bill. As with 'freight collect bills' the agent needs to satisfy himself that freight has been paid before releasing the goods.

Bills of lading are most usually issued for carriage from one port to another. In liner trades 'through transport' or 'house to house' bills may be issued. Under such documents the owners liability is much extended and will cover inland transport as well as the sea voyage. Where the agent is responsible for the issue of bills of lading particular attention must be paid to the place entered as the discharging port. If the agent inadvertently enters an inland destination or a port where the vessel is not scheduled to call, he could be laying the shipowner open to a duty to deliver the cargo to that place.

So far we have considered the bill of lading as a paper document. This is its most usual form, there are however attempts to introduce paperless transport systems with the bill of lading taking on an electronic identity. No doubt this will become commonplace in time and may eventually replace the paper bill of lading. Taking into account the various roles of the bill of lading and especially its function of a negotiable instrument there would appear to be many obstacles to overcome before the paper bill becomes obsolete.

Where a cargo is being shipped to a named known consignee or receiver and there is no need for the title to the cargo to be transferred then a non-negotiable document known as a 'way bill' might be used in place of a bill of lading.

BILL OF LADING

TO BE USED WITH CHARTER-PARTIES
CODE NAME: "CONGENBILL"
EDITION 1978
ADOPTED BY
THE BALTIC AND INTERNATIONAL
MARITIME CONFERENCE (BIMCO)

Conditions of Carriage.

(1) All terms and conditions, liberties and exceptions of the Charter Party, dated as overleaf, are herewith incorporated. The Carrier shall in no case be responsible for loss of or damage to cargo arisen prior to loading and after discharging.

(2) General Paramount Clause.
The Hague Rules contained in the International Convention for the Unification of certain rules relating to Bills of Lading, dated Brussels the 25th August 1924 as enacted in the country of shipment shall apply to this contract. When no such enactment is in force in the country of shipment, the corresponding legislation of the country of destination shall apply, but in respect of shipments to which no such enactments are compulsorily applicable, the terms of the said Convention shall apply.

Trades where Hague-Visby Rules apply.
In trades where the International Brussels Convention 1924 as amended by the Protocol signed at Brussels on February 23rd 1968 – the Hague-Visby Rules – apply compulsorily, the provisions of the respective legislation shall be considered incorporated in this Bill of Lading. The Carrier takes all reservations possible under such applicable legislation, relating to the period before loading and after discharging and while the goods are in the charge of another Carrier, and to deck cargo and live animals.

(3) General Average.
General Average shall be adjusted, stated and settled according to York-Antwerp Rules 1974, in London unless another place is agreed in the Charter.

Cargo's contribution to General Average shall be paid to the Carrier even when such average is the result of a fault, neglect or error of the Master, Pilot or Crew. The Charterers, Shippers and Consignees expressly renounce the Netherlands Commercial Code, Art. 700, and the Belgian Commercial Code, Part II, Art. 148.

(4) New Jason Clause.
In the event of accident, danger, damage or disaster before or after the commencement of the voyage, resulting from any cause whatsoever, whether due to negligence or not, for which, or for the consequence of which, the Carrier is not responsible, by statute, contract or otherwise, the goods, Shippers, Consignees or owners of the goods shall contribute with the Carrier in general average to the payment of any sacrifices, losses or expenses of a general average nature that may be made or incurred and shall pay salvage and special charges incurred in respect of the goods.

If a salving ship is owned or operated by the Carrier, salvage shall be paid for as fully as if the said salving ship or ships belonged to strangers. Such deposit as the Carrier or his agents may deem sufficient to cover the estimated contribution of the goods and any salvage and special charges thereon shall, if required, be made by the goods, Shippers, Consignees or owners of the goods to the Carrier before delivery.

(5) Both-to-Blame Collision Clause.
If the Vessel comes into collision with another ship as a result of the negligence of the other ship and any act, neglect or default of the Master, Mariner, Pilot or the servants of the Carrier in the navigation or in the management of the Vessel, the owners of the cargo carried hereunder will indemnify the Carrier against all loss or liability to the other or non-carrying ship or her Owners in so far as such loss or liability represents loss of, or damage to, or any claim whatsoever of the owners of said cargo, paid or payable by the other or non-carrying ship or her Owners to the owners of said cargo and set-off, recouped or recovered by the other or non-carrying ship or her Owners as part of their claim against the carrying Vessel or Carrier. The foregoing provisions shall also apply where the Owners, operators or those in charge of any ship or ships or objects other than, or in addition to, the colliding ships or objects are at fault in respect of a collision or contact.

For particulars of cargo, freight, destination, etc., see overleaf.

The clauses of the Congen Bill

CODE NAME: "CONGENBILL" . EDITION 1978

BILL OF LADING

B/L N

TO BE USED WITH CHARTER-PARTIES

Shipper

Reference No.

Consignee

Notify address

Vessel   Port of loading

Port of discharge

Shipper's description of goods   Gross weight

(of which   on deck at Shipper's risk; the Carrier not
being responsible for loss or damage howsoever arising)

Freight payable as per

CHARTER-PARTY dated ....

FREIGHT ADVANCE.

Received on account of freight:

....

Time used for loading .... days .... .hours.

SHIPPED at the Port of Loading in apparent good
condition on board the Vessel for carr
Port of Discharge or so near thereto as she may safely get
specified above.

Weight, measure, quality, quantity, condition, contents and
known.

IN WITNESS whereof the Master or Agent of the said Vessel
the number of Bills of Lading indicated below all of this teno
any one of which being accomplished the others shall be voi

FOR CONDITIONS OF CARRIAGE SEE OVERLEAF

Freight payable at	Place and date of Issue
Number of original Bs/L	Signature

C.15   Printed and sold by
Witherby & Company Limited, 32/36 Aylesbury Street,
London EC1R 0ET.

The cargo details on the Congen Bill

123

| Shipper | **BCL BOLT CANADA LINE LTD** |
| | CYPRUS |

| Consigned to order of | |

BOLT CANADA LINE
CONTAINER SERVICE

| Notify address | |

UK General Agents
MORLINE LTD.

* Local Vessel	* From (local port of loading)
(Ocean) vessel	Port of loading

Morline House, London Road,
Barking, Essex. IG11 8BB.
Telephone: 0181-507-6000
Telex: 889066/7

Port of discharge	* Final destination (if on-carriage)	Freight payable at	Number of original Bs/L

Marks & Nos.	Number and kind of packages; description of goods	Gross weight	Measurement

Particulars furnished by the Merchant

SHIPPED on board in apparent good order and condition, weight, measure, marks, numbers, quality, contents and value unknown, for carriage to the port of discharge or so near thereunto as the Vessel may safely get and lie always afloat, to be delivered in the like good order and condition at the aforesaid Port unto Consignees or their Assigns they paying freight as per note on the margin plus other charges incurred in accordance with the Provisions contained in this Bill of Lading.

One original Bill of Lading must be surrendered duly endorsed in exchange for the goods or delivery order.

IN WITNESS whereof the Carrier has signed the number of original Bills of Lading stated above, all this tenor and date, one of which being accomplished, the others to stand void.

IN ACCEPTING THIS BILL OF LADING THE SHIPPER, CONSIGNEE AND THE OWNERS OF THE GOODS AND THE HOLDER OF THIS BILL OF LADING, AGREE TO BE BOUND BY ALL OF ITS CONDITIONS, EXCEPTIONS AND PROVISIONS WHETHER WRITTEN, PRINTED OR STAMPED ON THE FRONT OR BACK HEREOF.

* Applicable only when document used as a Through Bill of Lading.

| Place and date of issue |
| **LONDON** |
| Signed, for and on behalf of the carrier, BCL Bolt Canada Line Ltd., Cyprus |
| p.p. Morline Ltd. as Agents |

The cargo details on a Liner Bill

1. **Definitions**. "Carrier" means BOL LTD on whose behalf this Bill of Lading has been signed. "Merchant" includes the Shipper, the Receiver, the Consignor, the Consignee, the Holder of this Bill of Lading and the Owner of the goods. "Ship" includes any (substituted) vessel and any craft, lighter or other means of conveyance owned, chartered or operated by the Carrier used in the performance of this contract.

2. **Issuance of the Bill of Lading**. By the issuance of the Bill of Lading the Carrier

1) undertakes to perform or to procure the performance of the entire transport from place at which the goods are taken in charge to the place designated for delivery in this Bill of Lading;

2) assumes liability as set out in these Conditions.

3. **Carrier's Tariff**. The terms of the Carrier's applicable Tariff are incorporated herein, in case of any inconsistency between this Bill of Lading and the applicable Tariff, this Bill of Lading shall prevail.

4. **Paramount Clause**. In respect of any carriage by sea, this Bill of Lading shall have effect subject to the provisions of the Carriage of Goods by Sea Act of the United States, the Hague Rules, or the Hague-Visby Rules, as applicable, or such other similar national legislation as may mandatorily apply by virtue of origin or destination of the Bills of Lading which shall be deemed to be incorporated herein and nothing herein contained shall be deemed a surrender by the carrier of any of its rights or immunities or an increase of any of its responsibilities or liabilities under said applicable Act. If any term of this Bill of Lading be repugnant to said applicable Act to any extent, such term shall be void to that extent, but no further.

5. **Jurisdiction**. Any claim or dispute under this Bill of Lading shall be determined, at carrier's option, by the law and courts of the country where the carrier has his principal place of business, or the country of shipment or delivery.

6. **Methods and Routes of Transportation**. The Carrier is entitled to perform the transport in any reasonable manner and in reasonable time, by any reasonable means, methods and routes, whether or not the most direct or advertised or customary route, via any port or places in any order whatsoever and for whatsoever purpose visited, together with other goods of every kind dangerous or otherwise whether stowed on or under deck, Vessels may sail with or without pilots, undergo repairs, adjust equipment, drydock and tow vessels in all situations

7. **Transhipment and Forwarding.** Whether expressly arranged beforehand or otherwise the Carrier shall be at liberty to carry the goods to their port of destination by the said or other vessel or vessels either belonging to the Carrier or others, or by other means of transport whether by water, land or air according to the applicable tariff and conditions and may discharge the goods at any place for transhipment, tranship, land or store the goods either on shore or afloat and reship or forward the same. The Carrier in making arrangements for any transhipping or forwarding vessel or means of transportation not operated by this carrier shall be considered solely the forwarding agent of the shipper. The responsibility of the Carrier shall be limited to the part of the transport performed by him on vessels under his management and no claim will be acknowledged by Carrier for delay, damage or loss arising during any other part of the transport even though the freight for whole transport has been collected by him.

8. **Discharge and Delivery**. Notwithstanding any custom of the port the Carrier may discharge immediately without previous notice when the ship is ready, no matter where she is lying, as fast as ship can, directly as the goods come to hand at or on to any quay, or overside in lighters or in any other way, that the carrier may elect, at all hours day and night, Sundays and holidays included, regardless of the state of the weather at the risk of the Merchant. The expense incurred after discharge of the goods to be borne by the Merchants. If the Merchants for whatsoever reason fail to take delivery of the goods according to these conditions or if they fail to do so promptly, the Carrier is at liberty to put them into lighters, warehouses, customhouses and the like, all at the risk and expense of the Merchants. These conditions apply, if otherwise is not provided in the tariff. See cl., – Additional Conditions.

9. **Lighterage**. The carrier in arranging for lighters or other transportation between ship and shore, does so as the Merchant's agent and for account and risk of the goods.

10. **Optional Stowage and Deck Shipment**. The carrier is at liberty to stow the goods in poop, forecastle, deckhouse, shelterdeck, spare bunkers or any covered space commonly used in the trade for the carriage of such goods and when so stowed shall be deemed for all purpose to be stowed under deck. Where the goods are stated herein to be received and/or shipped as deck cargo such goods are carried at Merchant's risk in which case the Carrier shall be under no liability for any loss or detention thereof, or damage thereto, arising from any cause whatsoever. The Carrier shall be entitled to carry the goods on deck in containers, trailers, transportable tanks or similar articles of transport used to consolidate goods whether they are stowed there by him or Merchants. The Carrier is not required to give notice to the Merchant of any stowage and carriage as provided in this clause. These goods (container, etc.) carried on deck be treated as if they were stowed under deck and the Hague and York-Antwerp Rules as incorporated herein shall be applicable to them,

11. **Hindrance, etc., Affecting Performance**. If in the event of restraint of authorities, epidemic, quarantine, ice, labour troubles, strikes, lockout, congestion and any other causes beyond carrier's control the goods cannot be discharged at the port of destination without risk to ship and cargo, the carrier is entitled to land the goods at one of the nearest ports of call where possible at Merchant's risk and expense and to inform the Merchant thereof, if possible.

12. **Extent of Responsibility**:

1) The Carrier shall be liable for loss of or damage to the goods occurring between the time, when he received the goods into his charge and the time of delivery.

2) The Carrier shall however be relieved of liability for any loss or damage if such loss or damage arose or resulted from:

a) act, neglect or default of the master, mariner, pilot, or the servants of the carrier in the navigation or in the management of the ship;

b) the wrongful act or neglect of the Merchant;

c) compliance with the instructions of any person entitled to give them;

d) the lack of or defective condition of packing in the case of goods, which by their nature, are liable to wastage, or to be damaged when not packed or when not properly packed; unless the package had been carried out by Carrier;

e) handling, loading, stowage or unloading of the goods by the Merchant or any person acting on behalf of the Merchant;

f) inherent vice of the goods;

g) insufficiency or inadequacy of marks or numbers on the goods, covering or unit loads; except where they are required to be affixed by the Carrier;

h) strikes or lockout or stoppage or restraint of labour from whatever cause whether partial or general;

i) any other cause or event which the Carrier could not avoid and the consequences whereof he could not prevent by the exercise of reasonable diligence;

3) Where under sub-clause 2 the Carrier is not under any liability in respect of some of the factors causing the loss or damage, he shall only be liable to the extent that those factors for which he is liable under this clause have contributed to the loss or damage.

4) The burden of proving that the loss or damage was due to one or more of the causes. or events. specified in a, b, c and i of sub-clause 2 shall rest upon the Carrier.

13. **Limitation of Responsibility**. For the sea carriage the carrier shall in no case be liable in an amount exceeding USD 500 per package or unit or the equivalent of that sum in other currency, unless value declared on the Bill of Lading, for the carriage by any other means of transport or during any services incident to the through transportation of the goods every carrier shall be liable according to the law, rules and conditions applicable to the respective means of transport or by other contractors under the pertinent sub-contracts. The merchant agrees that each container/pallet loaded/stuffed by him, his servants or agents (including the entire contents thereof) shall constitute one package for all purposes including limitation of carrier's liability. If the container shipped is not the property of the carrier, the merchant warrants that said container is actually seaworthy packed and in every way fitted for loading, stowing, carriage and discharge.

14. **Notice of Loss**. Unless notice of loss of or damage to the goods and the general nature of it be given in writing to the Carrier at the place of delivery before or at the time of the removal of the goods into the custody of the persons entitled to delivery thereof under this Bill of Lading, or if the loss or damage be not apparent, within three consecutive date thereafter, such removal shall be prime facie evidence of the delivery by the Carrier of the goods as described in this Bill of Lading.

15. **Time Bar**. The Carrier shall be discharged of all liability under the rules of these conditions unless suit is brought within one year after delivery of the goods, or in the case of total loss of the goods, the period shall begin with the moment when goods should have been delivered.

16. **Defences for Servants, etc**. The defence and limits of liability provided for in this B/L shall apply in any action against the Carrier for loss or damage to the goods whether the action be founded in contract or in tort, also in any action against a servant agent, or independent contractor, unless it is proved that the loss or damage resulted from an act or omission of the Carrier or of this person done with intent to cause damage or recklessly and with knowledge that damage would probably result.

17. **Inspection of Goods**. The carriers shall be at liberty at the place of loading or discharging as well as during the voyage to have the contents inspected in order to ascertain the weight, measurement or value for the purpose of verifying the freight basis and their correspondence to their description. If on such inspection it is found that the declaration is not correct it is agreed that a sum equal to five times the difference between the correct figure and the freight charged or to double the correct freight less the freight charged, whichever sum is the smaller shall be payable as liquidated damages to the Carrier notwithstanding any other sum having been stated on the Bill of Lading as freight payable if otherwise is not provided in the tariff.

18. **Sealed Goods**. The carrier shall not be responsible for the shortage of or damage to the goods arrived at the destination in good containers or other similar receptacles duly sealed by the Shipper and for the goods delivered in other safe and good packages without any signs of opening (unsealing) them during the carriage in case of Merchant's failure to prove that such shortage of or damage to the goods occurred through the fault of the Carrier.

19. **Lien**. The Carrier shall have an absolute lien on goods for any amount due under this contract and for contribution in respect of general average and for salvage to whomsoever due, including costs of recovering the same and storage fees, and may enforce such lien, in any reasonable manner which he may think fit. If on sale of the goods the proceeds fail to cover the amount due and the cost and expenses incurred, the Carrier shall be entitled to recover the difference from the Merchant.

20. **Description of the Goods**. The Merchant shall be deemed to have guaranteed to the Carrier the accuracy, at the time the goods were taken in charge by the Carrier, of the description of the goods, marks, numbers, quantity and weight (including gross weight of the container or any other receptacle) as furnished by him, and the Merchant shall indemnify the carrier against all loss, damage and expense arising or resulting from inaccuracies in or inadequacy of such particulars. The Merchant is liable for the said incorrectness according to clause 17. The right of the Carrier to such indemnity shall in no way limit his responsibility and liability under this Bill of Lading to any person other than the Merchant,

21. **Freight and Charges**.

1) Freight shall be deemed earned on receipt of the goods by the Carrier and shall be paid in any event, goods lost or not lost, and not to be returned.

2) Freight and all other amounts mentioned in this Bill of Lading are, at the option of the Carrier, to be paid in the currency named in this Bill of Lading or any other currency acceptable to the Carrier.

3) All dues, taxes and charges or other expenses in connection with the goods shall be for the account of the goods.

4) The Merchant's attention is drawn to the stipulations concerning currency in which the freight and charges are to be paid, rate of exchange, devaluation or revaluation and other contingencies relative to freight and charges in the relevant tariff conditions. If no such stipulation as to devaluation or revaluation exists or is applicable the following clause to apply: "If the currency in which freight and charges are quoted is devalued or revalued between the date of the freight agreement and the date when the freight and charges are paid, then all freight and charges shall be automatically and immediately changed in proportion to the extent of the devaluation or revaluation of the said currency".

5) The Merchant shall reimburse the Carrier in proportion to the amount of freight for any costs for deviation or delay or any other increase of costs of whatever nature caused by war, warlike operations, strikes, government directions or force majeure.

22. **Stowage in Containers by the Carrier**. The Carrier may stow the goods in containers and has the right without notice to the Merchant to carry them in closed containers.

If the goods accepted for shipment are packed into containers by or on behalf of the Carrier, the Carrier's responsibility for the goods commences at the moment of reception of the goods by the Carrier and ceases when the goods are discharged out of the container at the port of destination.

The Carrier shall during the whole period from such loading until unloading be entitled to the benefit of all privileges, rights and immunities contained in this Bill of Lading.

23. **Merchant-packed Containers**. Where any container, transportable tank, flat or pallet and other receptacles accepted for transportation has not been filled, packed or stowed by or on behalf of the Carrier, the Carrier shall not be liable for any loss of or damage to its contents and the Merchant shall cover any loss or expense incurred by the Carrier if such loss, damage or expense has been caused by:

1) negligent filling, packing or stowing of the container, and any other receptacle.

2) the contents being unsuitable for carriage in container or any other receptacle.

3) the unsuitability or defective condition of the container or any other receptacle. unless they have been supplied by the Carrier and when the unsuitability or defective conditions of the container were not apparent upon reasonable inspection at or prior to the time when the container or any other receptacle was filled, packed or stowed.

24. **Special Container**. If the goods are stowed by or on behalf of either the Carrier or the Merchant in special container with refrigeration or heating units the carrier does not accept any responsibility for the functioning of such containers not owned or leased by the Carrier.

25. **Repositioning of Containers**. Where containers owned or leased by the Carrier are unpacked at the Merchant's premises, they are jointly and severally responsible for returning the empty containers with interiors brushed and clean to the port or place of discharge or to the point or place designated by the Carrier, his servants or agents within the time prescribed by the Carrier's Tariff. Should a container not be returned within the prescribed time the Merchant shall be liable for any demurrage, loss or expenses which may arise from such non-return.

26. **Heavy or Bulky Goods**. Pieces or packages weighing two tons each and upwards or of exceptional bulk or length or if awkward for vessel's tackle or gear shall be loaded and discharged at Merchant's risk and cranage and any other extra expenses shall be unless otherwise agreed, for account of the goods.

27. **General Average**. General Average to be adjusted at any port or place at the Carrier's option and to be settled according to the York-Antwerp Rules 1974 with amendments 1990, this covering all goods carried under deck and the containers and etc. carried on deck. The Amended Jason Clause as approved by BIMCO to be considered as incorporated herein. Average bond with values declared therein to be signed, also sufficient security to be given as required by Masters or agents.

28. **Incorporated Clauses**. This Bill of Lading shall be subject to all conditions of the port clauses customarily included in liner Bill of Lading for the port at which the goods are discharged as fully as though such clauses were printed herein.

The Both-to-Blame Collision Clause, War Risks Clauses Voywar 1950 as approved by BIMCO are fully and specifically incorporated in this Bill of Lading.

29. **Demurrage/Detention Clause**. Free time/demurrage and detention charges according to respective clause of tariffs in force.

30. **Dangerous Goods**. Before the goods of dangerous or damaging nature and radioactive material are tendered for shipment, the Merchant shall inform in writing the Carrier, Master or Agent of the Vessel, of their exact nature of danger, indicating the precautions to be taken, give the name and address of the sender and receiver and distinctly mark the nature of the goods on the surface of the package or packages, as required by the International Maritime Dangerous Goods Code and applicable statutes or regulations and in addition on each container, flat, trailer, etc. A special stowage order giving consent to shipment must be obtained from the Carrier. The Merchant will be liable for all loss, damage, delay or expenses, if the foregoing provisions are not complied with.

31. **War Clause**. No contraband of war shall be shipped. Vessel shall not be required, without the consent of Owners, which shall not be unreasonably withheld, to enter any port or zone which is involved in a state of war, warlike operations, or hostilities, civil strife, insurrection or piracy whether there be a declaration of war or not, where vessel, cargo or crew might reasonably be expected to be subject to capture, seizure or arrest, or to a hostile act by a belligerent power (the term "power" meaning any de jure or de facto authority or any purported governmental organization maintaining naval, military or air forces).

The clauses of a Liner Bill

Delivery Orders

Closely allied to bills of lading, 'delivery orders' are used when the goods covered by one bill of lading are sold to several different buyers. The party selling the goods will present the bill of lading to the agent in exchange for the requisite number of delivery orders each detailing a part of the cargo. Where the bill of lading in question is a 'freight collect' bill, the agent must either collect full freight from the bill of lading holder on issuance of the delivery orders or he may, with the shipowners authority collect proportional amounts of freight when the delivery orders are exchanged for the goods.

Cargo Manifests

A cargo manifest is a detailed list of cargo carried on a ship under each bill of lading. For bulk cargoes the manifest and the Bill of lading can be identical, for liner ships however they are much more complex. Then there will be a separate list for cargoes from each load port further divided for each discharge port. On modern large liner ships there may be hundreds or even thousand of entries on the manifest.

Manifests may include details such as freight amounts paid and to be collected. Unlike bills of lading which are limited in number and which are for the shippers use the manifest can be produced in unlimited numbers to be used by owners, agents and port officials to record and identify what cargo is being carried and to whom it belongs. Copies of the manifest will be delivered to many different parties as soon as possible after they have been prepared, including Customs, and Port Authorities at the loading port and also to the agent and stevedore at the discharge port. The discharging port agent will need to provide additional copies to Customs and other officials there.

The Agent at the discharge port will use the manifest to determine who are the receivers of cargo *'en route'* to his port so that he may keep them advised of the vessels impending arrival. He will also be able to identify any cargo for which freight is to be paid and to make sure that money is handed over before delivering the goods.

Customs at the discharging port will use the manifest to identify any goods which are subject to special import procedures or duties. It will also be used as a check list against which individual Bills of Lading are checked off as the goods are removed and duties paid. Because they detail all the cargo on the ship for the port on one document they are invaluable in compiling statistics of goods imported and exported.

The discharging stevedore will probably receive a version of the manifest which does not include freight details as they should be kept confidential. The stevedore will use the manifest to make preliminary arrangements for planning the equipment and space needed to discharge and store the cargo.

Stowage Plans

The manifest may contain all details of the cargo carried but it does not detail where on the ship it is loaded and whether or not other cargo is stowed on top of it. The document which does this is the stowage plan. Stowage plans may be produced as diagrams or for more simple cases merely as text. Stowage plans are invaluable to the stevedores and are quite useful to the agent as they allow him to give receivers of cargo some idea of how quickly his cargo is likely to be discharged.

On container ships where containers are placed in stacks and rows the stowage plan is often referred to as the bay plan. Each space or bay is allocated a unique number which allows the placing of a container to be immediately identified. This system allows hazardous goods to be kept segregated and in case of emergency easily located by crew and shore emergency teams.

PORT AGENCY

Chapter Seven

OUT OF THE ORDINARY

Unusual Events

The usual business of the agent can be predicted with some certainty, involving in the main routine tasks. There may however be occasions when ships or their crew are involved in unusual events. When unusual events occur at a distance from the shipowner's base the agent will undoubtedly be called upon to assist.

This section attempts to deal with some of those unusual events which occur most frequently.

Passengers, Deserters and Stowaways

Unwanted passengers are one of the shipowner's worst nightmares, causing major legal problems and expenses.

There are basically three ways in which unscheduled passengers can be taken on board ships. Firstly and least trouble are persons rescued from the sea following shipping disasters. In such cases the agent will need to do no more than inform the immigration authorities and the consular officials of the ships flag state and of the rescued persons.

Not so welcome are persons rescued from the sea following escape attempts from wars or their after effects. Although such unfortunate people might well be considered as refugees the fact is that many countries do not welcome them. Despite the efforts of the United Nations High Commission for refugees there are always countries which for one reason or another actively discourage attempts by refugees to enter their country. Such discouragement may be enforced by either heavy fines on ships, refusal to allow ships to enter ports or unwarranted quarantine restrictions forcing the vessel to be idle for long periods of time.

In the face of official sanctions the agent is powerless to do more than give prior warnings to his owner principal if problems are anticipated.

The worst kind of unauthorised passengers are stowaways. Stowaways may come on board surreptitiously or by secreting themselves in the cargo. The ships crew are responsible for attempting to prevent stowaways boarding the vessel, but they are seldom successful in stopping a determined stowaway. When agents are working in ports where stowaways regularly gain access to vessels, they should advise the master to be extra vigilant, maybe offering to arrange special watchman. Problems with stowaways are at their worst when the ship enters port after they have been discovered. The agent must be prepared to assist the master in dealing with the appropriate authorities in order, hopefully, to arrange the removal of the stowaways. Usually the owner will also seek assistance from his P&I Club.

Today virtually every shipowner has some form of P&I cover. P&I clubs offer mutual assistance to shipowners for those events which are not covered by normal insurance policies. Each P&I club has a world-wide network of correspondents, local experts in marine and legal matters. It is in all agents interests to get to know local P&I correspondents and to work with them in solving the owners problems.

The attitude of a large number of countries to stowaways is worse than that towards refugees. Unlike refugees, stowaways are not likely to arouse public sympathy. The result is that many authorities flatly refuse to allow them to leave the ship. Depending upon the normal employment of the vessel it is not unheard of for stowaways to spend months or even years on board. However unwelcome these people are the shipowner still has a duty to feed and look after them. They must be guarded when the ship is in port to prevent their escape which could lead to fines against the ship. In ships with limited accommodation and small crews resentment can soon build up and it is not unknown for stowaways to fall victim to physical abuse. Very occasionally stowaways are murdered or thrown overboard by ship's crews.

Additional persons arriving on ships do provide minor problems for the agent but persons missing on departure of the ship can be much more of a headache.

Deserters from the crew can leave the vessel short-handed or missing essential personnel. All ships have a minimum safe manning level prescribed by the ships flag state. Recognising that sickness or injury can deplete crews most ships carry a few extra men, although in today's harsh economic climate some owners do try to save money by sailing with their bare minimum crew. The minimum safe manning certificate will also identify what officers must be on board the vessel at all times, should a desertion leave the vessel deficient in men. Replacement crew will need to be engaged. Occasionally permission will be given by port or flag state authorities for the vessel to continue on its voyage if the owner has made arrangements for the missing men to be replaced at a more convenient port.

Desertions are usually discovered as the vessel is preparing for sailing, the agent must report the matter to appropriate authorities without delay. The authorities involved will include immigration, consular officials of the ship's flag state and possibly local police. Should the owner arrange for immediate replacement the agent may need to obtain visas more quickly than normal.

Although not technically deserters it is not unknown for passengers on cruise ships or supernumeraries on cargo ships to be missing when the ship is ready to leave. The agent will still need to inform immigration and consular officials including those of the missing persons home state.

The reporting of any deserters or missing person may just be the beginning of a long term headache for the agent. All deserters unless they deserted in their own country can be considered as illegal immigrants.

Immigration rules in most parts of the world make the shipowner responsible for fines, and costs involved in the detention and repatriation of deserters. There are a number of nations where this liability is extended to the agent, in such cases the agent should try to obtain some form of guarantee from the owner to pay all costs incurred.

Deserters sometimes turn out merely to have been prevented for whatever reason from arriving back at their ship in time. The agent will have to advise all concerned and either repatriate him or arrange transport to the vessel at the next port as the owner wishes.

General Average

'General Average' is an ancient concept aimed at compensating a party who has lost goods or incurred expenses as a result of a voluntary act aimed at saving a voyage in time of peril. The compensation comes from contributions from all parties with an interest in the voyage.

The principles of general average are laid down in the various versions of the York-Antwerp rules, the last of which was in 1994.

Despite the technological advances in ship design and the safety features required under regulations sea transport is still subject to numerous risks and dangers.

Some of these dangers will result in loss of, or damage to the ship and its cargo. Where the loss or damage is purely accidental as in deck cargo being swept away in high seas for example there is no question of general average. The unlucky victims of the loss will almost certainly be able to recover the loss through his insurance cover.

Occasionally the voyage will be imperiled and only a deliberate act of sacrifice will be able to save the voyage. If for example deck cargo is not swept away but is shifted causing the vessel to list dangerously, it may be necessary to jettison the cargo in order to prevent a capsizing of the ship.

General average need not involve physical loss. Expenditure aimed at saving the voyage can also result in a general average situation. Taking the previous example the master may decide that the vessel can only be made safe by restowing the cargo. To do this he will need to put into port or refuge for the necessary work to be done. This will involve expenses for entering the port and the cost of restowing the cargo.

It has already been said that for any act to give rise to general average it must be done voluntarily. This is not the only precondition. Aside from the voluntary nature the act must be successful in that it removes the peril and allows the voyage to continue. Finally the peril itself must be real and not imagined. An imagined peril may be difficult to conceive but an example would be where the master believes that some cargo in the holds is on fire. Should he put into port and discharge cargo only to find that there is no fire the expenses incurred would not be covered by general average. Involuntary acts and imagined perils do not remove entirely the likelihood of compensation. The losses involved may still be recoverable from the victim's own insurance policies. Losses of this nature are referred to as 'particular average'.

Having seen what gives rise to general average a explanation of how it works is in order. The object of general average is to compensate the party that has suffered losses by way of contributions from all the parties to the venture.

This is achieved by calculating the actual loss and then proportioning it according to the financial interests of all parties, including the party which has suffered the loss. At first it may appear strange that someone who has suffered should contribute towards the fund established to compensate him. Further reflection would lead to the proper conclusion that if he did not contribute, he alone would not suffer as all the other parties would have lost to the value of their contributions.

The following simple example of a general average calculation should give a better understanding of the principles.

Let us suppose that a vessel valued at $2,500,000 is carrying a cargo for three different receivers. The total cargo is valued at $4,000,000 and is split amongst the receivers as follows:-

A has cargo valued at $750,000, B's cargo is valued at $2,250,000 and finally C has cargo worth $1,000,000.

During a severe storm the cargo shifts and in order to prevent the ship from capsizing the master orders some deck cargo valued at $250,000 to be jettisoned. It so happens that all this cargo belongs to A. With the ship still listing dangerously and the deck cargo in an unstable condition the master heads for the nearest port where the cargo is restowed and the vessel is able to proceed and to complete the voyage. The port costs incurred by the ship totaled $30,000 including the costs of restowing.

Assuming that all the rules of General Average have been satisfied and that none of the expenses incurred by the ship were for extraneous items the calculations involved are as follows:-

The total value of the voyage is the sum of the ship and the cargoes.

Value of ship	$2,500,000
Value of cargo A	750,000
Value of cargo B	2,250,000
Value of cargo C	1,000,000
Total	6,500,000

Each party contributes towards each loss dependent on its share of the total.

The contributions towards the cargo loss are:-

Shipowner	$\dfrac{2,500,000}{6,500,000}$	x	250,000	=	96,153.85
Cargo A	$\dfrac{750,000}{6,500,000}$	x	250,000	=	28,846.15
Cargo B	$\dfrac{2,250,000}{6,500,000}$	x	250,000	=	86,538.46
Cargo C	$\dfrac{1,000,000}{6,500,000}$	x	250,000	=	38,461.54

Using the same formulae the contributions of each party towards the owners expenses are calculated as:-

Shipowner	$\dfrac{2,500,000}{6,500,000}$	x	30,000	=	11,538.46
Cargo A	$\dfrac{750,000}{6,500,000}$	x	30,000	=	3,461.54
Cargo B	$\dfrac{2,250,000}{6,500,000}$	x	30,000	=	10,384.62
Cargo C	$\dfrac{1,000,000}{6,500,000}$	x	30,000	=	4,615.38

The calculations in real life are made by specialist 'average adjusters'. The simplest cases are those involving easily proved loss such as jettisoned cargoes. The most complex cases are those involving calls at ports of refuge, additional works, and repairs or salvage costs.

Leading the list of the average adjusters tasks is that of weeding out unconnected expenses, which the owner would have incurred in any event. Then he has to establish the true values involved, as soon as general average is declared there is a noticeable tendency for those who have suffered to exaggerate their claims whilst those who have not will attempt to assign lower values to their ship or cargo.

Further complications arise if the vessel is carrying cargoes for large numbers of shippers such as might happen on modern liner ships where hundreds if not thousands of bill of lading holders are involved.

The agents role in general average cases will involve informing all parties and assisting in the distribution and collecting of general average bonds. General average bonds are forms which must be completed by each of the parties with an interest in the voyage. These bonds contain, or are accompanied by, a written undertaking to pay over the required sum when all the calculations are complete. Until a cargo owner has returned a bond he will not be entitled to take delivery of his cargo. It is not sufficient for the bond to be signed by the cargo receiver only. The owner will be looking for some form of security which generally takes the form of an endorsement by the cargo insurers or a bank guaranteeing payment of sums approved by the average adjuster.

The average adjuster may prefer to control the distribution and receipt of bonds himself as the agent is entitled to charge an additional fee for this work. Both the average adjusters fees as well as the agents are included into the incurred costs and as such are ultimately apportioned between the shipowner and cargo interests.

Whoever attends to the distribution and collection of the bonds the agent must ensure that the cargo is safely looked after until the bond is returned.

Very few cargo owners will have experience of general average and the concept may be completely alien to them. The agent should be able to explain the principal of general average, and should advise the cargo owner to take the matter up with the cargo insurers.

Occasionally an owner will declare general average when he is not entitled to do so. However the agent is obliged to act as if the owner did have the right until a court of law rules to the contrary.

Cargo Claims

When a shipowner enters into any form of contract to carry goods for freight he has to accept a certain amount of responsibility for looking after the cargo whilst it is in his care. Whenever he fails or appears to fail in this duty the inevitable result is a claim from the owner or insurer of the cargo to compensate for losses involved.

Cargo claims fall broadly into one of two categories namely shortages or damages. The agent's obligation to protect the owners interests means that he will frequently be called upon to assist in determining the validity of claims or investigating the circumstances which gave rise to them.

Taking each category in turn we shall look at ways in which the agent may become involved.

Shortage Claims

Shortages are clearly the difference between the loaded quantity and that which is finally discharged. Some bulk cargoes suffer a degree of natural wastage during transit and a percentage of

PORT AGENCY

weight or volume is usually allowed for by the trade to cover this effect. Where any shortage is inside this allowed figure there is little likelihood of a claim. For any cargo which is not subject to natural wastage the reason for the shortage has to be established.

For bulk cargoes, likely causes are differences between the weighing methods used at the loading and discharge ports. Lorries or rail wagons bringing cargo to and from the ship usually pass over a weigh bridge after which the weight of the vehicle is deducted to give the figure of cargo on the lorry or wagon. Occasionally the weigh bridge may be defective or mistakes occur when calculating the weight of cargo. The owner facing a claim may ask the agent at either port to obtain official proof of the accuracy of the equipment. Faulty equipment may also be the answer when metering devices are used in silos or pipelines.

Another method of determining weight of bulk cargoes is by way of draft surveys. Here a specialist surveyor will attend the vessel and make note of the vessel's draft in ballast and again when loaded. After studying the vessels documents and displacement scales it will be possible to calculate the quantity of cargo loaded or discharged. Due account is taken of the bunkers, water and stores on board at both ends.

Weather conditions can also cause discrepancies between intake and out-turn figures, lightweight bulk cargoes loaded in windy conditions almost always result in some quantity of cargo being blown away from the ship or lorry receiving the cargo.

Methods of cargo handling are a frequent cause of shortages, even when lorries are weighed accurately methods such as grab discharge result in a greater or lesser degree of spillage. Quay sides are nearly always covered with a layer of cargo when grabs are used for discharging. Spillage is always more of a problem when cargoes are discharged to the quay and subsequently reloaded to lorries before being weighed.

The agent attending a bulk vessel should make notes of any circumstances he feels may result in claims against the ship and draw the master's attention to any excess spillages. The master should of course already be well aware of any problem but may ask the agents help in protesting to the stevedores and cargo owners.

Shortages of non-bulk cargoes can occur when mistakes are made in tallying of the cargo at either end. At the loading port the ship's cargo mate should be making his own count and discrepancies between his and the tally clerk's figures can be checked or noted for special investigation at discharge. Where the mistakes occur at discharge ports it can be more difficult to check, especially when the cargo may have already left the port when the mistake is discovered.

The above examples have all assumed that shortages can be the result of innocent mistakes or poor handling but of course many shortages arise from theft or deliberate attempts to defraud. Theft by ships crews and dock workers are by no means uncommon although the advent of containerisation has reduced the extent of the problem for general cargoes.

The agent can assist in preventing theft by shore workers by arranging for tallies to take place alongside the ship and not when goods are delivered from or to warehouses. This is particularly important at the discharge port as the practice in many places is for the official tally to take place only when goods are delivered out from the port, this may be days or even weeks after the discharge actually took place.

Shortages of cargo at a port can occur when the vessel is discharging at more than one port. In such cases cargo can be mistakenly discharged at the wrong port. The agents task here is to attempt to trace the cargo by contacting the other discharge ports and enquiring if the cargo has been overlanded at any of them. Agents at ports where cargo has been overlanded should of course attempt to find the proper destination of the cargo. Sometimes the cost of transporting such cargo to its proper destination may be so expensive that the shipowner will pay the cargo owner the value of the cargo and request the agent at the port where it was landed to find a local buyer to offset his losses.

Having discussed shortages it is worth mentioning that inaccuracies in weighing systems can have the opposite effect and overages may occur at the discharge port. Where the owner can establish that the higher figure is the true tonnage he may be entitled to extra freight for the difference in cargo carried. There are many cases of the shipper of cargoes deliberately understating the tonnage loaded in an attempt to get some cargo carried free. Apart from being fraudulent this practice is incredibly dangerous as it can result in the ship being overloaded. Masters should of course check that the loadline is not submerged but at **naabsa** berths or when weather conditions make checking difficult the fact that the ship is overloaded can go unnoticed.

Damaged Cargo

Damage to cargo can occur at almost any time and may even exist before the cargo is loaded. The ship's cargo mate should be checking the condition of cargo loaded and noting damages on the mate's receipt for later inclusion into the bill of lading. Damage however, is not always immediately apparent and may only become obvious at a later time and place. Where the damage is caused by bad handling by stevedores the burden of responsibility is dependent on the terms of carriage. Even when cargo is carried on F.I.O. terms some contracts call for the stevedore to be considered as employed by the shipowner.

The agent should report to the master any instances of bad handling which he witnesses occurring, whether in or alongside the ship or at more remote places such as a warehouse or transit shed.

When cargo is damaged during loading the master may call for the damaged cargo to be taken out of the ship and repaired or replaced before he is willing to sign a bill of lading. Although he may well be within his rights such actions do occasionally cause friction with cargo interests. The agent may make some diplomatic attempts to resolve the situation but may well need to report the matter back to the owners for instructions.

Many cargoes are quite prone to damage by handling techniques and all agents should make enquiries about likely problems if they are themselves unfamiliar with the cargo. At the very least they can then ensure that the stevedore has the right equipment to be able to handle the cargo without causing unnecessary damage. Where specialised handling equipment is used the agents at both loading and discharge ports should find out what type of gear is available to be used at the opposite end as there are often several different methods of handling and stowing specialised cargoes. In some cases totally different equipment makes discharge of the cargo difficult without the use of the same equipment by which it had been loaded. Should the stevedore be lacking specialised equipment the agent must make this known to the shipowner at the earliest opportunity so that alternatives can be explored.

One of the most common causes of damage to cargo after damages caused by bad handling or stowage is that of wet damage. When a ship arrives at the discharge port and the hatches are opened revealing wet cargo the cargo owners first reaction is to claim that the ship has leaking hatches. This may or may not be true and careful investigation into the causes of the damage must be carried out. Firstly the agent needs to ensure that the damaged cargo is placed aside in an area which is dry and suited to the storage conditions necessary for that type of cargo. The shipowner will then arrange for tests to be carried out to determine if the damage has been caused by fresh or salt water. Salt water damage is a strong indicator that the ships hatches are indeed deficient in some way. It is not conclusive proof as there have been cases of cargo stored on open quays in winter having been contaminated by road salt used to melt snow and ice on the quay.

PORT AGENCY

Where it is proved that the damage was by fresh water the likely source of the damage has to be further investigated. The agent at the loading port may be able to establish that the cargo was stored in the open prior to loading or that the shed in which it was stored was leaking.

Some cargoes which may appear dry are often not. Packaged timber is an example of a cargo which is commonly stored in the open for quite long periods. When it has been exposed to rain or snow it may at certain times be dry on the outside but wet and icy inside the packs, during the sea voyage the ice will melt and a lot of wet damage can occur.

In order to assist their owner principals, agents should make it a part of their service to monitor cargoes at the port before the ship's arrival if at all possible. They would then be in a better position to advise the owner and master of matters which may cause problems later. A note should be made and kept with the ships file of any likely events which could give rise to a claim of any sort.

Wet damages can occur also during loading and discharging operations which are carried out in bad weather. Usually the master will close the hatches if there is a threat of rain or snow. Where the shipper or receiver wishes to complete operations quickly, perhaps to avoid demurrage, and demands that work continues the agent will need to assist the master in passing a letter of protest to the stevedores and the cargo owners. Wet damage is also a threat when a ship experiences extremes of temperature during a voyage. Condensation occurs when a ship travels through low temperatures from and to warmer and more humid areas, and some cargoes may 'sweat' releasing moisture in certain conditions. Where the damage is attributable to such causes the owner will need to show that adequate ventilation of the cargo was made during the sea voyage.

Another cause of frequent claims is that of contamination of the cargo. This can be a particular problem in bulk trades both liquid and dry. The owner can quite easily protect himself when it can be proved that the contaminant had not been carried in the ship prior to the loading of the cargo. It is much more difficult when the contaminant material may well have been carried in the ship shortly before the carriage of the cargo concerned. The agents may be helpful in such instances by informing the owners of any likely sources of contamination at the ports. It is not unknown for shore silos to have residues of previous cargoes remaining in them or for automated systems to malfunction allowing mixing of cargoes from adjoining silos or tanks.

Damage claims need not concern damage to the cargo itself but may relate to the packing of the cargo. Many products such as steel, timber, plywood, bagged cargoes, palletised cargoes and such like commonly suffer damage to the packaging during handling and transportation. The packing of these products is done either to reduce handling costs or to contain and protect the cargo. When the packaging is damaged additional costs and or losses might occur. It is therefore essential to repack them as soon as possible. The agent should arrange with the stevedores to put any damaged packs aside during discharge so as to ascertain the extent of the problem. When the ship's master and the cargo owners have been able to agree the extent of the problem the cause has to be discovered. This may require the services of a surveyor to investigate handling methods and the quality of the packing. When it has been established where the damage occurred the liability for re-packing costs will be decided and the cargo repacked.

In the usual course of events concerning any form of cargo claim the agents role will be to assist in establishing when, where and how the damage occurred and passing information to the owner which may assist him in protecting himself. Beyond this the agent should always give prior information to shipowners if he believes that a particular problem exists with regard to the cargo at his port. This should include information about cargo handling techniques, tallying procedures, ability and impartiality of local surveyors as well as warnings about particularly troublesome cargo owners.

Fumigations

Sometimes a ship or a cargo may become infested with pests which are detrimental to the health of the crew and to cargoes. Pests may be introduced into the ship from within cargoes carried or they may be naturally present at ports which the ship visits during the normal course of events. However they have been introduced, there exists the need to eradicate them.

The most usual way to do this is by means of fumigation. Fumigation involves the use of various chemicals alone or in combinations to be introduced into the ships holds and accommodation as necessary. The area being fumigated must then be closed off for a period to allow the chemicals to take effect. Many of the fumigants used today contain chemicals harmful to human health and it will then be necessary to take the crew off the ship for the time in question.

When a fumigation is deemed necessary the port agent may be asked to arrange for it to be carried out by a local contractor. If there is a need for the crew to leave the vessel the agent will almost certainly need to make arrangements for their accommodation ashore.

The cost of the fumigation and indeed the expenses for the crew will need to be paid for in due course. Where the vessel is operating on a liner service the costs will almost certainly be for the owners account, but for tramp vessels the liability will be decided by the charter party. When a fumigation is necessary, because a charterer has loaded contaminated cargo, the costs will normally be directed to the charterer.

Fumigations may sometimes be ordered by a port health authority. This is almost certain to happen when the ship has been affected by human disease, the cause of which or means of transmission can be destroyed by suitable fumigants. Official intervention also occurs when the ship is affected by insects or other organisms which may have detrimental effects on plants and livestock in the region of the port. Notable examples include woodboring insects and similar creatures, gypsy moths and Colorado beetles.

Collisions

Collisions with other ships and with objects fixed or floating occur quite frequently in and around ports, this is not surprising given that confined areas and manouevering of ships are ideal conditions for accidents to take place. Whenever a collision takes place the first thing a ships master will do after the situation is brought under control is to call in his P and I club's surveyors and representatives. They will need to attend in order to ascertain the damage to the ship and the object with which it collided, there will then follow preliminary investigations to discover the cause of the collision. When the collision is between the ship and a fixed object such as a jetty or lock gate it is not unknown for the port to try to claim that the damage is greater than it actually is, especially if they see a chance to repair or replace previously damaged and worn out structures and equipment.

When collisions have occurred and extensive damage has been done the parties suffering damage may demand that the other party puts up security to cover the estimated cost of repairs. Securities are usually arranged by the owners P and I clubs or insurers. In some ports ships will not be permitted to sail until adequate security has been arranged. Any collision will usually bring about an inspection by local port state control officials and if sufficiently serious an enquiry organised by the relevant authorities. When severe damage occurs to the ship the agent is attending, he may need to arrange emergency repairs, pollution prevention or medical attention for injured personnel.

The agent may be aware of navigational difficulties which are found to be contributory causes to a number of collisions, if this is the case he should of course pass on his knowledge to the master who may decide to delay arrival or sailing until the cause of the problem no longer presents a threat to safe navigation. Examples of this may be particular combinations of wind and tide when entering locks.

Very often the agent will be called upon to assist after a collision in obtaining statements from pilots and other witnesses. It is not the agents duty to determine the cause of the accident but he should disclose any relevant information to his owner or principal. The majority of work will be done by the ship owners P and I surveyors and correspondents. Depending upon the size and importance of the port involved these may or may not be local men. Where they have needed to travel any distance from the port they will require the assistance of the agent in arranging meetings and inspections.

Surveys

There are many reasons why an agent may be called upon to arrange surveys of one kind or another. Surveys are carried out by different organisations depending upon the type of survey being called for. To arrange a survey the agent need only contact the correct surveyor and agree the time and place that the survey is to take place. Surveyors rarely operate on an exclusive basis and it may be that the same surveyor has connections with insurers of both parties in an incident. Should he already have been retained by the other side the agent may be asked to find an alternative. Most agents will have a number of surveyors amongst their acquaintances and can quite readily arrange an alternative.

The matter of surveys has been touched upon earlier, but the following is a more detailed explanation of how and why some of the more usual surveys are carried out.

Damage Surveys

These are required when there has been damage to the ship, her equipment or an object with which the ship has collided. In the main these will be performed by the shipowners local P and I surveyor, there is every likelihood of a second surveyor representing the other party being in attendance. The P and I clubs will also send surveyors to inspect cargo damage allegedly caused by the ship.

Pre-shipment Surveys

There are certain cargoes which are prone to damage and deterioration during transportation. When they have contracted to carry such cargoes the prudent owner will arrange for the cargo to be carefully inspected prior to and during loading. This will be done by a specialist surveyor who can identify problems which an inexperienced crew member may miss. In addition to checking the condition of the cargo the surveyor will also make an inspection of the ships hold and cargo hatches. The shippers of the cargo may well arrange their own survey and where the two surveyors can agree their reports will be acceptable proof of the condition of the cargo at the outset of the voyage. Many subsequent cargo claims can be rejected on the basis of the pre-loading surveys.

The value of these surveys is such that for some cargoes, such as steel , the shipowners P and I club will withdraw cover unless the requisite survey has taken place. Some P and I clubs will even absorb the cost of the survey as an added service to the shipowner.

Classification Surveys

All ships are required to have certain certificates before they are allowed to trade. Most certificates are issued by the ship's classification society on behalf of the flag state authority. Some flag states do issue their own certificates but generally the work is delegated to either the national classification society or a foreign society of good standing. Certificates such as the safety equipment, safety construction, safety radio and loadline certificates are issued for a period unto five years subject to annual surveys. They may be extended by consular officials for a short time to allow the ship to travel to a port where the annual inspection will take place. Efficient owners will be aware of when inspections need to take place and will usually make their own arrangements for surveyors to attend. Occasionally the need for an inspection is either overlooked or changes to the ship schedule means that she is not in the appointed place at the right time. In such circumstances the agent may need to arrange for the survey to be carried out. There may not be a representative of the ship's classification society in the port in which case the owner and agent will need to investigate if the class society will accept an inspection by another class society. Most of the major classification societies are members of the International Association of Classification Societies (IACS) and are quite happy to accept a survey from another member. In other cases it will be necessary for the ships class society to make a formal request for another surveyor to attend. This can take time and, especially for vessels with short port stays, is best organised well in advance.

In order to remain classified with a society the ships hull and machinery has to be maintained to reasonable standards. Inspections take place either at specified intervals or on a continual basis. The owner will inform the class society of the ship's intended itinerary and the surveyor will initiate contact with the agents to arrange to meet the ship during a convenient port visit.

Ships which carry or intend to carry hazardous goods must have an additional certificate showing what class of goods can be carried. The issue of this type of certificate is done by a class society at the request of the flag state. Basically it requires that the ships Safety Equipment and Safety Construction certificates are in order and that the ship is supplied with certain additional equipment sufficient for emergencies which may arise when carrying any of the hazardous goods allowed by the certificate. These certificates can be required at short notice and the agent must be ready to obtain any of the specialist additional equipment required by the surveyor before the certificate can be issued.

Draught Surveys

This type of survey has already been mentioned as a means of determining the weight of cargo on board at loading and discharging ports. When asked to arrange a draught survey the agent will contact a local marine surveyor. Marine surveyors are usually master mariners or chief engineers who have decided to work ashore. An accurate draught survey requires proper determination of the ships draught when in ballast as well as true measurements of bunkers, stores, fresh and ballast water on board at both ends. Additionally the density of the water at the loading and discharging berth have to be taken into account. The agent must know in advance if a draught survey is to be made because no work can commence before the surveys are made otherwise their is no way of determining what the ballast or loaded draught is.

On and Off Hire Surveys

These surveys take place at the beginning and end of a time charter. Their purpose is to determine the condition of the ship at both times so that any damage which has occurred during the period of hire can be ascertained. The surveys will not only cover the condition of the ship but will also include matters such as cargo securing equipment and the quantity of bunkers on board. Most time charters call for joint surveys to be made with a surveyor attending from both sides. Occasionally the master will act as the owner's surveyor and on rare occasions the owner and the charterer will agree to accept a sole surveyor to attend. Various arrangements can be made concerning who is to pay for the surveys and the agent when asked to arrange such a survey should clearly establish who is going to pay the surveyor. On and Off hire surveys are usually carried out by local marine surveyors.

Arrest and Detentions of Ships

There is a difference between the terms arrest and detention although in the first instance the agents tasks will be similar under both. A ship is arrested with the intention of forcing the owner to settle some outstanding matter or to lose his ship if he fails to do so. Detention on the other hand is an official intervention preventing the ship from sailing until certain matters have been put right. A detention may lead to arrest if the owner does not act to settle the cause of the detention.

Although there are many different legal systems existing throughout the globe most of them are quite similar in respect of remedies available when money is owed by one person to another. The most extreme of the remedies is the seizure and sale of goods to the value of the sum owed. Ships are universally considered as goods belonging to the owner and are legitimate targets for such legal actions. The only difference between ships and other types of goods is that ships move internationally and so move from one legal jurisdiction to another. The means of obtaining legal detention of the vessel may be more difficult for the creditor under some systems than others. The initial step for any person intending to arrest a ship is for him to present his claim to the appropriate legal entity in the country where he intends to arrest the ship. Some legal systems will require that the matter has first been put to the legal system in the claimants own country and been accepted there. Supposing that his claim is accepted he will obtain a writ allowing him to apply for the vessel to be arrested as security for the debt owed to him. Some legal jurisdictions will not issue a writ until the owner has had a chance to refute the claim against him. The procedure in such cases is to issue a summons to the ship which gives them a period of time in which they must either pay the claimant, present a defence, or put up some form of security for the claim pending legal examination of it by an appropriate body. When a summons has been issued the ship is perfectly entitled to carry on as usual until the period allowed has expired. Should the shipowner choose to ignore the summons he will find that the writ will be issued

150

automatically and the ship is certain to be arrested on its return to the country in question.

Once the writ has been issued the claimant must wait until the vessel arrives at a port in the country which issued the writ or at a port in another country which is prepared to accept the writ as a valid reason for allowing the arrest of the vessel without further legal procedures.

The possible list of claimants seeking arrest of a ship includes bunker suppliers and shipchandlers, repair and maintenance contractors, port authorities and port service suppliers, cargo owners with claims against the vessel, the ships crew for wages owed, governments owed money by the owner, and agents and brokers for money due to them. Not all countries will allow a ship to be arrested for the full range of possible debts. Some countries are much more willing to allow arrests than others. Shipowners with problems soon learn to avoid the most lenient countries when operating their ships.

The actual arrest of the ship is usually carried out by a government department or an authorised representative. In Britain arrests are usually made by H.M. Customs and Excise officers acting on behalf of the Admiralty Marshal. In other countries the procedures may involve Coastguards, Harbour Masters or Water Police. The arrest procedure usually consists of a formal verbal arrest of the ship by the arresting officer followed by an attachment of a notice to the ship advising of the arrest. In former times in Britain the notice would have been nailed to the ships mainmast but today it is taped to a window on the bridge. The arresting officer has to inform the port authorities who should prevent the vessel leaving the port after it has been arrested. It is not unknown for arrested ships to slip out of port under cover of darkness without pilots or tugs and to prevent this the vessel may be ordered to a berth from which escape would be impossible or which is under strict supervision. Although the vessel is not permitted to sail from the port it is normal for cargo operations to continue until all the cargo on board is removed from the ship.

PORT AGENCY

Agents aware of the threat of an impending arrest should make the information known to the shipowners as soon as possible so that he can take necessary measures to avoid undue delay to his ship. The fact that someone is seeking to arrest a vessel does not mean that the owner is at fault. The reason for the arrest may be connected with debts unknown to the owner which have been incurred by a time charterer of the vessel, or the cause may have arose at a time when the vessel was owned by another party. The prudent agent will of course be careful to avoid incurring debts on behalf of the owner in case the owner is having solvency problems.

Once a ship has been arrested the responsibility to pay port charges incurred during the arrest period lies either with the arresting party or with the government of the state where the arrest took place. In some states the responsibility for crew welfare also passes to the arresting authority. Where this is the case they may order the repatriation of non-essential crew. Should the owner be unable or unwilling to remain responsible for the crew the authorities may ask the agent to continue attending the ship to attend to crewing and maintenance matters. There is no difference in attending to a ship on behalf of an authority instead of the owner except that the agent will need to separate out costs incurred for each party and to incur costs only if they have been previously agreed.

When a shipowner is in serious financial difficulties it will be almost certain that he owes money to people other than the party making the arrest. Once it becomes known that a ship has been arrested other creditors will appear to attach their own claims to the arrested ship. Some creditors may not actually join in the arrest of the ship but wait to see if the owner is able to raise sufficient funds to pay the arresting parties in full. Should the owner be successful in settling those debts the waiting creditor may then make his own arrest of the ship. The reason behind the waiting is to see how much money the owner is able to raise. If he had joined in earlier the owner may have become insolvent and would have been only able to pay a percentage of the claims.

The arrest of the ship ends when the owner either settles the matter for which the ship is arrested or the ship is disposed of under the directions of the arresting authority. Where the owner is able to free his ship from arrest the agent will be expected to arrange the sailing of the ship in the normal manner. The legal arguments connected with some of the causes for arresting ships may take months or even years to settle. Ships that have been languishing under arrest for long periods will undoubtedly need some mechanical attention and supplies before they are again ready to put to sea. When a ship is disposed of by judicial sale the proceeds are applied to settle the various debts on the basis of their priority. First covered are the expenses of the authority which allowed the arrest of the vessel, next the claims of the crew for wages are settled, then will come any secured debts such as mortgages and only after that the unsecured debts of the owner due to any party which participated in the arrest.

An arrested ship need not remain under arrest if the owner or his insurers, usually a P&I club are willing to offer acceptable guarantees of payment in the event that the legal process finds in favour of the claimant.

It was said earlier that detentions are official interventions designed to make the owner comply with certain conditions. Ships are detained usually for two types of problems, the first is to ensure payment of funds. Many countries have laws which call for money to cover port costs and agency fees to be received before the vessel is allowed to sail. Agents at ports where such laws apply have a duty to inform the owner of the fact in good time. Transfer of money through the worlds banking systems is extremely variable and just because the system in the agents own country may allow transfers to be made within hours he should not assume that similar conditions apply in the shipowner's home state. The agents duty also is to ensure that sufficient funds have been requested. The owner who transmits the requested sum will not be happy if at the point of sailing he receives a sudden demand for more money as the agent had under-estimated the costs of the call.

153

Detentions also occur when the vessel is inspected by port state control officials who discover deficiencies with the vessel, her crew or equipment. Port state inspections have become much more rigorous in recent years and large numbers of ships are detained each year. The agent cannot influence the outcome of inspections but he can advise owners of what types of ships, flags and problems are being targeted in his port. If deficiencies are discovered the owner will need the agents assistance in arranging repairs, spares or new equipment. Once a ship has been detained for safety or environmental reasons it becomes a regular target for inspectors in other ports until conditions on board the ship are deemed to have reached acceptable standards.

Chapter Eight

THE AGENT AND MONEY

Costs and Fees

We have seen that when a ship enters a port a number of services such as pilotage, tugs etc. along with the port dues will have to be paid for. For a small ship these charges may amount to a few hundred pounds only but for a large tanker or passenger ship the costs may well reach tens if not hundreds of thousands of pounds.

The costs paid are to third parties are the agents disbursements for which the agent may require to be placed in funds prior to the ships arrival at the port. The agents own fees and expenses are not disbursements and the agents should not include these into demands for advance payment, although many do.

Agency fees are relatively modest and except for the very smallest vessels will not be a major item in the vessels final port account. Unfortunately shipowners attempting to contain costs who find difficulty in reducing port charges will often select the agents charges as a soft target and demand rebates from customary agency fees.

In view of the small return for his services the agent will quite rightly expect to have satisfactory arrangements in place for the payment of disbursements and fees. This can be arranged in any of several ways.

Where the agent is entrusted with the collection of freight the owner may permit payment of disbursements from the money collected. This arrangement is satisfactory providing the freight due is sufficient to cover costs and providing the agent is able to collect the freight without too much difficulty.

When no freight is to be collected the shipowner may simply transfer money directly to the agents bank account. Today's technology allows even international transfers to be made with little delay except when one of the parties is domiciled in one of the more remote, less advanced parts of the globe.

Owners may sometimes request charterers to pay funds to the agent directly and reduce the amount of freight accordingly. Some charter parties which call for freight payment on or after discharge, contain clauses covering payment of disbursements at loading ports. Usually they permit the charterer to charge a commission of about 2.5% on any funds advanced. If the charter party or freight contract requires freight payment at loading port then no commission will be charged for payments made after the due date for freight payment.

Shipowners and agents who have long standing relationships and trust may make other arrangements perhaps using letters of credit from which the agent can draw funds against either pro-forma or completed accounts. An agent who has a good credit rating with port authorities and contractors may be able to extend credit to the owner for a short period.

Agents, and indeed all those connected with shipping, have always feared the delinquent shipowner who refuses or is unable to meet his liabilities. Port authorities have to some extent eased their problems by introducing by-laws and regulations seeking to make the agent liable in the event that the shipowner defaults. the argument behind this is that the agent is in the best position to know the owners status and having accepted an agency appointment the agent should take some responsibility for the action of his principal. There is some logic in this argument, but the fact that a supplier of services is in a position to refuse service without adequate guarantees or in the case of a port authority able to prevent a vessel from sailing, should be a more effective safeguard than relying on the agent to make good the owners shortcomings.

Any agent who, having accepted an appointment, cannot persuade the owner to make satisfactory arrangements for payment should be prepared to relinquish the appointment rather than face the prospect of taking on such a risk. When no funds have arrived before the vessel sails, particularly when requests for funds have been made in good time, the agent needs to decide whether or not to advise the port authority and request them to prevent sailing.

Of course business failures and delinquency are not confined to shipowners. There are probably as many cases of agents who having received advance funds have not paid the suppliers and subsequently become insolvent. The fact that the shipowner has paid money in advance to an agent who has failed, is not a defence against claims from the unpaid creditor. In order to avoid arrest of his ship the shipowner is invariably obliged to pay the costs a second time direct to the supplier.

Agents must avoid using funds received from one shipowner to pay the costs of other owners who have not provided the agent with the funds to cover their own costs.

Ideally agents should open separate client accounts for each owner/principal and use money only for the benefit of the proper party. They must also take steps to make clear the identity of the owner of the money and to ensure that it cannot be mistaken for the agents money in the unfortunate event of the agents liquidation.

When considering disbursement accounts and the securing of funds to cover them it must be remembered that some suppliers are prepared to offer discounts or rebates to prompt payers and regular users. Whenever the agent is successful in obtaining such rebates he is legally obliged to pass on the cost savings to the owners. There is one exception to this rule and that applies when the agent has not received advance funds from the owner but is prepared to settle an account quickly from his own resources in order to secure a discount.

Almost all agents in liner trades and many of those attending tramp vessels may be asked to collect freight on behalf of the shipowner. Should the agent be prepared to accept this task he must ensure that he does everything possible to secure payment in good time and must never allow release of goods or documents against mere promises to pay.

Collection of freight is an additional task over and above the normal duties of the Port Agent. It is usual for the shipowner to allow the agent a commission of between 0.5% and 2.5% of the amount collected. Liner agents may enter in agreements whereby they receive only commissions and no actual agency fee as such.

When an agent collects freight on behalf of the owner he is commonly allowed to retain sufficient amounts to cover the disbursements of the vessel. The balance however should be treated in the same way as advance funds in a separate bank account away from the agents own monies.

The agents own services are paid for by the inclusion of an agency fee. This subject was covered in Chapter 2 but it is worth repeating that in order to avoid disputes the level of remuneration should be agreed before the agent undertakes any work.

Chapter Nine

SHIP TYPES

Introduction

The design of ships has constantly evolved over centuries but major revolutionary changes appeared firstly when wooden hulls were replaced by metal and again when engines began firstly to augment and eventually replace sails.

More recently cargo handling methods have influenced design and produced specialised container and Ro Ro vessels. Navigational routes, and political events like the Suez crisis and Middle East wars have resulted in the VLCC and ULCC'S used to carry oil round the Cape of Good Hope rather than through Suez.

Economies of scale have also affected vessel sizes in surprisingly different ways. Standard size vessels have been replaced by much larger ships for ocean trades with feeder vessels concentrating and distributing cargoes before loading and after discharge of the ocean carrier. Distribution by feeder allows small cargoes to be delivered economically to facilities outside of the main ports of the world.

This situation is clearly illustrated in Northern Europe with its handful of hub-ports such as Felixstowe, Rotterdam, Le Harve and Hamburg serving the deep-sea vessels and the huge number of sea-river vessels operating between sea ports and deep inland along the Rhine, Seine, Scheldt and Elbe rivers of Western Europe and the Sainaa and Russian canal systems. Cargoes in vessels using the Russian system can be carried as far as the North Iranian ports of the Caspian sea.

The following plans and details are representative of ship types which are commonly used today and may be seen in most ports. Variations, particularly in size, will be encountered for most of the basic types.

Sea-River Vessel

Rhine or Bilsma traders and Russian sea-river types, Not usually exceeding 4500 - 5000 dwt. Mostly used for the carriage of bulk products such as grain, coal and timber. A large number can also carry containers and may have been specially designed for this trade.

Hatches are generally large and holds boxed shape. Hulls are mostly flat bottomed allowing vessels to go easily aground at low water, a common occurrence in spite of the shallow draught normally found in this type of vessel. The shallow draught does restrict sailing in heavy seas and high winds and it is not unusual for vessels to suffer long delays at anchor or by sheltering to avoid the worst weather. This problem is recognised by classification societies who inevitably place restrictions on the trading limits of these vessels, additionally vessels will not be permitted to sail more than a set distance, usually 50 or 100 miles from a port or place of refuge. The majority of these vessels do not venture beyond North European and Mediterranean waters.

Very few of these vessels are geared and so must be loaded and discharged by shore cranes. Very manouvarable, they are often built with twin engines each driving independent propellers, bow thrusters and usually burn diesel or gas oil, of which they will consume about 5 tonnes per day. Although their manoeuvering capabilities are good they are not the fastest of ships with speeds averaging 10-11 knots. This is not a problem as the voyages for such ships tend to be of relatively short distances.

Timber Carriers, Small Bulk Carriers

These vessels are generally from 2000 dwt upwards to 15000 dwt. They are used for much longer voyages than the sea-river types and do not have the navigational restrictions imposed on those vessels. They are much deeper draughted even when of the same dwt as a sea river vessel and do not have the flat bottoms associated with that type.

This type of vessel is well suited to long range trades in higher value commodities and will be appreciably faster than the smaller types. An average speed would be around 14-15 knots with a daily consumption of about 15-20 tonnes of fuel oil.

Due to their greater sailing range these vessels may often find themselves in ports less well equipped than those in the main trading centres of the world. For this reason they often have cargo handling gear of some type on board. This may be simple derricks capable of handling only 2 - 5 tonnes or possibly proper cranes of larger capacity.

The configuration of the hatches and holds of this type of vessel are similar to the smaller ships described above. The box shaped holds make them versatile ships capable of carrying general cargoes and unit loads as well as bulk.

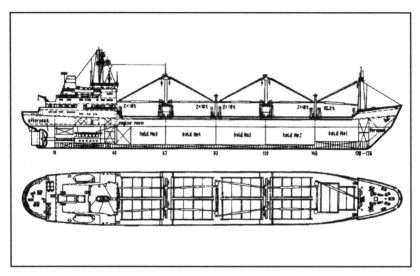

15,000 tonne Bulk/Timber Carrier

Large Bulk Carriers

Bulk carriers are the main types of vessels used for the long distance transport of raw materials. They all tend to be somewhat similar in basic design having accomodation and engine rooms aft of a quite high number of hatches. The reason for having many hatches is primarily one of safety in that it reduces the effects of any shifting of the cargo, there are also operational reasons such as allowing part cargoes to be loaded along the full length of the ship, this improves trim and stability and allows for the loading of several different grades or commodities.

Within the basic design of the bulk carrier are several recognised sub types. Some of these relate to the size of the ship and areas where she is able to operate. Smaller vessels of between 25,000 and 50,000 dwt are known as 'handy size' , 'Panamax' refers to vessels up to 80,000 tonnes with dimensions suited to the Panama Canal. Under normal conditions this would be a length of 289.5 metres, a beam of 32.3 metres and a draught of up to 12.04 metres. Beyond the Panamax vessels up to 17 metres draught are known as Suemax, the largest size able to transit that canal. Larger vessels up to 180,000 dwt are known as Cape size, this name recognises the fact that to move between the Atlantic and Indian Oceans they must pass the Cape of Good Hope at the tip of Southern Africa. Finally there are very large bulk carriers up to 250,000 dwt commonly known as VLBC's.

All of the larger bulk carriers will carry coal and ores but grain and higher value commodities are not normally carried in the VLBC class. The speed of all the various larger bulk carriers is between 12 and 14 knots.

With larger vessels popularity decreases with size as the number of ports able to accept the very largest vessels is extremely limited. They do of course find employment and some are specially commissioned for specialist trades.

Apart from size other sub-types of bulk carriers include 'self-trimming' and 'self-unloading'.

Self-trimming ships have holds with an octagonal cross section. The slope at the top is designed to reduce the tendency of cargo to shift. Bulk cargoes are usually loaded by hoppers, spouts or elevators along the centre line of the hatch, this results in the cargo in the hold resembling an elongated pyramid. The sloping sides mean that there are few if any empty spaces along the sides of the hold which could allow the cargo to shift. The sloping construction need not be confined to the sides of the hold but can also be present at the fore and aft bulkheads of each cargo space. The bottom slope improves the discharge rate as the cargo slides down the sides of the hatches towards the centre where it can be more effectively grabbed from the ship.

Self-unloading bulk carriers incorporate conveyor belt devices which can be positioned when the hatches are open to discharge to either side of the vessel. The savings which can be achieved as a result of the quicker discharge rate of self-unloaders compared to conventional bulkers more than offsets the expense of installing the equipment.

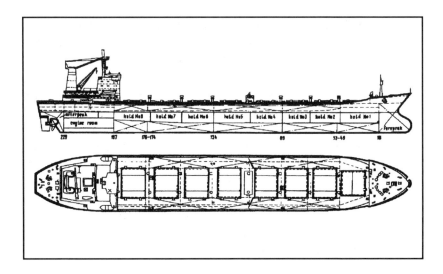

60,000 dwt Bulk Carrier

General Cargo Ships

Many of the smaller vessels described above are considered as general cargo ships for registration and classification purposes even though they are mostly used for the carriage of bulk cargoes.

Some ships are designed for the carriage of what is traditionally considered as general cargo, namely bagged, cased, drums, pallets as well as loose items of various sizes. In order to accommodate a whole range of different types of cargo they need to have several cargo compartments so they are usually built with at least four holds and more than one deck. Occasionally ships are built with tank capacity suitable for the carriage of products such as vegetable and fish oils and with one or more holds being refrigerated to allow the carriage of chilled produce. The majority of ships will be found within a range of 12-18,000 dwt although the full range of sizes is from 6000 dwt up to 25000 dwt.

The general cargo tween decker will invariably be equipped with a range of cargo gear from derricks and cranes with a capacity of 5 tonnes through to 'jumbo' derricks or heavy lift cranes able to lift more than 50 tonnes. These type of vessels are particularly suited to trading to ports in developing nations where investment in shore cargo handling equipment and containerisation has not yet reached the levels of the more developed states. In anticipation of future improvements in this position the old concept of tween deckers has undergone some radical changes over recent years and designs have been developed to take advantage of more modern cargo handling methods. The holds of newer ships have been configured so as to readily adapt to the carriage of containers. In the so called 'multi-purpose' vessels a Ro Ro ramp is also incorporated into the design of the ship.

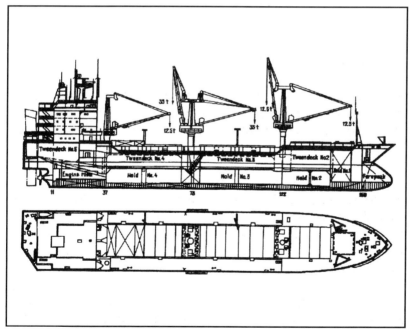

Multi-purpose General Cargo Ship With Ro Ro Capability

Bulk cargoes are also frequently carried in general cargo ships although the speed of loading and discharging cannot be compared to purpose built bulk carriers.

Container Carriers

The introduction of containers into shipping revolutionised the ways in which cargo was handled. From the original metal box the container itself has developed so that today specialised types of containers exist for all manner of cargoes which would once have been thought of as not suited to containerisation. There are for example tank containers which consist of a tank similar to those of road tankers suspended within a framework. Tank containers allow for any type of liquid cargo to be carried, some are specially lined for carrying sensitive or dangerous goods. Open top containers allow cargoes higher than the standard height to be put in a container, they are also used for goods which must be loaded into or taken out of the container by conveyor belt or grabs. Flat racks are designed so that when empty the ends can be folded down to allow several to be carried in the space occupied by one ordinary container. The only common element in the different types of containers is that they are of a recognised standard size and have a standard fitting at each corner, beyond that only human ingenuity is a limiting factor in their design and application.

The inherent security of containerised cargoes as well as the rapid turnaround in ports ensured that container ships would soon become the most suitable vessels for liner trades.

The success of containers in liner services has lead to larger and larger vessels being introduced. The capacity of early ships was measured in hundreds of TEUs but on the major routes today this has increased to thousands. The original ships are now used mostly as feeders for the larger modern vessels. The whole ideology of container traffic is speed and today's container ships can certainly claim to be the equivalent of the old clipper ships with vessels capable of speeds up to 25 knots or more.

Older container vessels often share features common in the smaller bulk vessels such as box holds and large hatches. Some ships are operated as 'conbulk' ships able to carry either containers or bulk cargoes depending on the market situation. The latest designs though are generally cellular. A cellular container vessel has built in cell guides which partition the ship in a honeycomb fashion. The containers are slotted into the guides and do not require further securing.

Most container ships have the ability to carry refrigerated containers connected to reefer points on the vessel. Refrigerated containers are similar to standard containers but as the name suggests they incorporate a refrigerating unit allowing the carriage of frozen and chilled goods.

Determining the correct positioning of containers in the holds and on the deck of container ships is a skilled task. The stability of the ship can be compromised, and safety when carrying hazardous goods adversely affected by the incorrect stowage of containers.

In liner trades the owner generally has a stowage co-ordinator whose job is to plan the positioning of cargo as bookings are taken. Before the ship begins to load he will have prepared a stowage plan in which the precise position of every container to be loaded is pre-determined. In today's age of technology many of these plans are prepared using computers and specialist software which may or may not be duplicated on board the vessel. Even so the ships officers will need to check the plan to ensure that due account has been taken of bunkers and ballast etc. on board. The ships crew and the stevedore will make careful checks to ensure that no container is wrongly positioned. Even under such scrutiny mistakes occur and containers may have to be restowed.

Ro Ro

Ro Ro is an abbreviation for 'Roll-on Roll-off'. Specially designed to accept wheeled traffic Ro Ro is another quick turn round concept. Speed is an essential element in Ro Ro services because the use of trailers means that cargo space is used very inefficiently. To overcome this freight revenues have to be higher than other ships of a similar size. There are many categories of Ro Ro ships. Aside from obvious candidates such as vehicle ferries the purpose built car carrier with several moveable decks is also a Ro Ro. There are several liner services operating either large purpose built Ro Ro vessels or multi-purpose ships having some Ro Ro capacity which carry road haulage vehicles. Some of these services will also carry accompanying drivers, because of the distances involved these can not be considered as ferries which are generally considered as short sea services. Ro Ro ships do have a niche in the tramp market for the carriage of military and agricultural machines sold in large batches and not suited for containerisation. Ro Ro vessels operating on liner services may be equipped with mafi trailers. These are similar to road trailers but are part of the vessels cargo handling system. Empty trailers are left at a port to be loaded with general cargoes whilst the vessel is at sea. On the return of the vessel the trailers on board are taken off and the pre-loaded trailers pulled on to the vessel by tractor units known as tug-masters. The discharged trailers are unloaded after the vessel has sailed and then reloaded with fresh cargo to await the vessels return.

All Ro Ro ships must of course have some type of ramp allowing the cargo to be driven on and off. The number and position of the ramp or ramps varies from ship to ship according to their prime purpose. Ships on ferry services usually have two means of access. In this way cars and trucks can be driven on to the ship at one port and driven straight off at the other end without the need to turn round or be reversed off the ship. In the ferry trade the ramps are usually positioned at the bow and the stern. Bow ramps are more complex structures than stern ramps and normally include a hinged section which lifts up or opens out in front of an internal watertight door. This is an essential element due to the need for the bow of the ship to be tapered. Stern ramps on the other hand can be and usually are more simple because there is no need to shape them for dynamic purposes. Both bow and stern ramps have a disadvantage in that they require the vessel to berth at an angle of 90 degrees to the quay. There is an increased risk of collision when manouevering and for cargo vessels it means that shore cranes cannot be used for loading deck cargoes of containers when working Ro Ro cargoes through the ramp. For these reasons the most common position of the ramp for Ro Ro cargo ships and multi-purpose types is on one or other of the stern quarters. On the quarter the ramp is angled allowing the ship to berth side on to the quay with the ramp projecting at an angle of about 45 degrees behind the ship. Ro Ro ships with two or more decks will be equipped with fixed or movable internal ramps or elevators to allow access to each deck.

One problem to be considered when working Ro Ro vessels is the angle at which the ramp is inclined to the quay. This angle is constantly changing as cargo is loaded or discharged increasing or decreasing the draft of the ship. There are also variations to the angle caused by the distance between the water level and the quay. This distance alters due either to tides at tidal berths or depth of water in enclosed docks. The water in enclosed docks can change with the opening and closing of lock gates.

There are a few ships which although not strictly Ro Ro do have a ramp of sorts in the side of the ship. These vessels known as side access vessels are used mostly in specialist trades such as the carriage of newsprint and woodpulp. The side access allows forklift trucks and other wheeled cargo or equipment to be driven on to an elevating platform inside the ship. The platform is raised or lowered to give access to the required deck. The ship can be berthed so that the side doors are positioned alongside covered quay spaces and thus allowing the ship to be loaded or discharged in rain and snow, conditions which would prevent the working of a ship with hatches on deck.

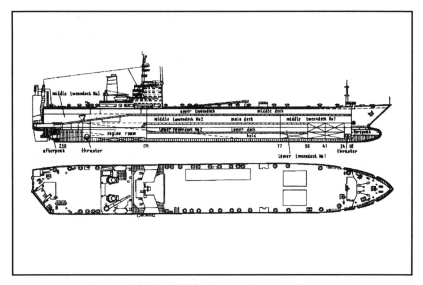

Large RoRo With Stern Quarter Ramp

LASH Ships

LASH is an anacronym for Lighter Aboard SHip. Along with other similar design such as BACAT (Barge Aboard CATamaran) they are a novel concept allowing the transport in one outer hull of several small lighters or barges across major oceans. The lighters or barges may be fitted with their own propulsion units or they may be towed. At the beginning of the sea voyage the small craft are positioned and secured inside the main hull which is essentially no more than a large floating self-propelled dock. At the destination the small craft are taken out of the main hull and continue their journey in quieter waters.

This method of transportation allows small lots of many different types of cargo to be loaded into and discharged from the barges at facilities along rivers and canals inaccessible to the mother ship.

The first system of this type was known as Sea Bee which gives the impression of a busy hard working ship. In fact the true name was C.B. which stood for Combat Battalion and identifies the U.S. military origin of the concept. The small lighters and barges

170

were to be used as landing craft for troops and equipment. The first system was in fact paid for by the Government and leased out for commercial purposes until required.

Despite its attractions as a distribution system it has one major drawback. The barges themselves are expensive and many are required to ensure that the mother ship has a constant supply of loaded craft to carry. Unlike containers the barges cannot be used for inland transport away from waterways so the system is not supported by industries with no access to river or canal berths.

Refrigerated Ships

Generally referred to as 'reefers' they are designed for the rapid carriage of foodstuffs such as fruit, vegetables, meat and fish. In outward appearance reefer ships are little different from any other general cargo vessel. The main difference is in the speed at which the ships are designed to operate. Shippers of chilled produce need to ensure that their cargoes are delivered to their destination as rapidly as possible to reduce the risk of deterioration. Consequently they are prepared to pay high freight rates for ships which have been built with engines capable of speeds twice that of general cargo ships and with equipment designed to keep the cargo at optimum temperatures in a controlled environment. Temperature control is a vital element in reefer transport. Whereas meat and fish need to be carried at temperatures below freezing, fruit and vegetables may well be ruined if the temperature is so low as to freeze them.

Reefer ships are generally employed on services from the fruit producing areas of the tropics to the main consumer markets in Europe and North America, meat is carried to the same destinations from New Zealand and South America and fish cargoes are carried world-wide.

When there is a lack of demand for reefer ships they can be used to carry more conventional cargoes since there is little if any difference in the configuration of cargo holds of reefer and general cargo ships. The prolonged use of a reefer vessel for conventional cargo is usually avoided because of the need to achieve high freight to pay for the additional equipment built into reefer vessels.

Passenger Ships.

There are a number of different categories of passenger ships, their construction and employment depends upon several factors. The advent of cheap passenger air transport has all but killed off the passenger liner ships. Today the most glamorous use to which passengers ships are put is in the cruise market. The cruise market has many levels ranging from short, cheap, basic journeys around small areas of interest such as the Greek Islands and the Mediterranean to world wide cruises of three months or more on new built luxurious ships with entertainment, dining and leisure facilities able to exceed that of many of the worlds cities.

What ever class of passenger the cruise operator is aiming at cruise ships can be very demanding upon the agents appointed to attend them. The stay in port is short with most calls lasting less than a day. Requirements though are many, the amount of fresh water and provisions consumed on board the larger ships is quite astounding so there will be a constant stream of trucks delivering to the vessel during her stay. Waste disposal facilities suitable for the size of the ship will need to be arranged whilst unusual requests from the ship will have the agents searching the local Yellow Pages attempting to locate anything from a fruit machine engineer to a piano tuner. The agent will be expected to handle mountains of mail both to and from the ship along with spare parts and equipment essential to the ship.

Cruise ships may be most peoples idea of what constitutes a passenger ship but by far the most common type are ferries of one sort or another. The organisation of ferry operators offices means that few ferries are attended by independent agents.

From a safety aspect passenger vessels represent the best and worst equipped of operated vessels. Already required by SOLAS to be constructed to high standards and to carry so much additional equipment, highly publicised disasters such as the 'Herald of Free Enterprise' and the 'Estonia' have been prime reasons for the introduction of new legislation and the ISM code. These measures have been accepted by major maritime countries but often not enforced in some developing nations where accidents involving overcrowded and ill maintained ships still continue to claim many lives.

Tankers

From the largest ships afloat, the giant supertankers engaged in global carriage of crude oil, down to the smallest coastal tanker of less than 1000 dwt all tankers are designed with one consideration in mind. The carriage of bulk liquids requires ships which carry them to be constructed in such a way as to reduce the risks of a cargo which cannot be made immobile in the tanks. Moving cargoes make ships unstable and liable to capsize. In tankers the effects of movement are reduced by making each cargo tank much smaller than the holds of dry cargo vessels. There is no loss of space in this because it is achieved by dividing the ship longitudinally into at least twice as many compartments as a dry cargo ship and by dividing each of these into three or more sections athwartship.

The large tankers of today are a legacy of the political instability in the Middle East from 1950 onwards. Before then, to carry crude oil from the Gulf to Europe by any route other than Suez would have been unthinkable. The closure of the Suez canal meant a re-routing of ships via the Cape. The additional costs pushed up the price of oil so much that a solution had to be found. The practical answer was to build bigger ships capable of carrying much larger cargoes. These ships were too large to pass through the Suez after it was re-opened but with the capital which had been invested operators continued to trade with them. At the same time the USA moved from being an exporter of oil to a nett importer so demand for larger vessels increased. Soon

173

vessels of 250,000 tonnes and later over 300,000 tonnes were being built.

Today's VLCC (very large crude carriers) and ULCC (ultra large crude carriers) are used purely for the carriage of crude oils whilst smaller tankers are used mainly for carriage of other bulk liquids including refinery products, chemicals, vegetable oils, molasses and wine.

The high risk of pollution from tankers means that these are subject to more rules and regulations on construction and operation than dry cargo vessels. The relative small size of the individual cargo compartments coupled with the small size of deck openings means that tankers are inherently more rigid than dry cargo ships hence their greater size. The tanks may be used for the carriage of cargo, ballast or both. Some tankers have tanks which are able to be used only for clean sea water ballast these segregated ballast tanks (SBT's) are designed to prevent the pollution which occurs when ballast becomes contaminated by cargoes. The use of SBT's is encouraged by disregarding them when calculating the vessels tonnages so reducing the figure on which port dues etc. are charged.

Tankers are not loaded and discharged by conventional means but by hoses connected to the ships manifold. The manifold is an interface between the shore hoses and the ships own pipelines, it is designed so as to accept several different types of fittings and sizes of hoses.

The ships pipelines are equipped with remotely operated valves which are opened and closed from the ships pump room. using this system cargo can be directed into or taken out of selected tanks as required for cargo separation or stability purposes.

The volatile gases given off by some cargoes which collect above the cargo in the tanks may be vented off or more usually displaced by inert gases from the ships engine exhausts. The opening of any tank top therefore present a safety hazard as well as a health risk so tankers must carry more fire fighting and breathing apparatus than on dry cargo ships. The inflammable and explosive nature of many cargoes is the cause of the strict conditions imposed by terminals as well as the siting of tanker jetties as far from the shore as possible. The conditions may include use of rubber safety footwear and prohibitions on mobile phones.

Tankers are rarely in port for long periods with pumping rates of 1500 to 5000 tonnes per hour for small vessels and around 10,000 achieved by the larger ships. Many ports do not allow tankers to navigate at night.

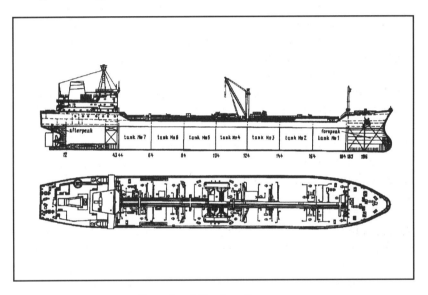

Standard Tanker Layout

Gas Carriers

There are about 1000 ships world wide designed and employed solely for the carriage of liquefied natural and petroleum gases. These gases are in the main butane, propane, vinyl chloride, propylene, ammonia, ethane and methane. Some are used as fuel others in manufacturing processes.

In order for gases to be liquefied they must either be refrigerated, stored under pressure or a combination of both.

The range of temperatures and pressures varies enormously between different gases. Butane for example can be carried at temperatures of +20 Celsius providing it is pressurised at 2 Bars. Methane (natural gas) cannot ever be carried at temperatures above -83 Celsius where 40 Bars of pressure would be required and is more normally carried at temperatures of -162 Celsius.

Most gas carriers used for a range of cargoes are able to reduce temperature to about -48 Celsius and to carry cargoes at about 5 Bars pressure, any decrease in one of these figures must be matched by an increase in the other. Students of physics will know that pressure is easier to maintain in safety in cylindrical or spherical structures where very high pressure is required.

Gas carriers which rely on pressure rather than refrigeration have large spherical tanks which protrude above the vessels deck.

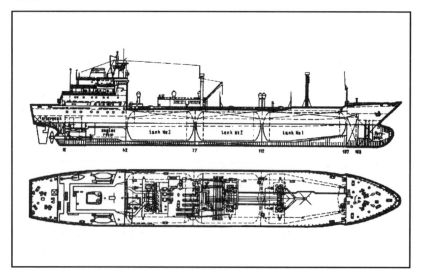

Gas Carrier - LPG Type

Ship Construction

Although there have been attempts to construct ships of many different materials virtually all ships currently working are made of welded steel. The shape of modern ships hulls has become much more streamlined but outwardly they are little different from those built 50 years ago. The internal construction is however very much different reflecting the trend towards safety and environmental protection. The original steel ships consisted of a single skin which once holed by collision or grounding would compromise the ship and almost certainly be a pollution hazard.

The first method of improving the safety aspect was the introduction of double bottoms. The double bottom is exactly as the name suggests a second skin extending the full width and length of the vessel. Double bottoms were conceived at a time when pollution was not the issue it is today. Shipowners and naval architects soon had the idea to utilise the space for ballast and fuel tanks, of course if the outer bottom was damaged the inner skin gave some protection against sea water ingress, but when fuel oil was carried there was a huge risk of pollution.

Following on from double bottoms a logical development was a second skin added to the sides of the hull. Again this came to be used for storage of ballast and fuel. The same problems existed as with double bottoms with regard to the environmental threat.

The importance which is now attached to environment protection has seen penalties for polluting rise to unheard of levels. As a consequence there is a move towards building vessels with genuine double hulls in which the void will not be used for storing any noxious substances.

The bulkheads between cargo holds must be able to withstand fires if the vessel is to be allowed to carry dangerous cargoes. These are rated according to the number of minutes and carry designations such as A15 A30 and A60. The rating of the bulkheads is important in determining what cargoes can be loaded into any given part of the ship.

Vessels which have cargo holds aft of the engine room may have a shaft tunnel in those holds. The shaft tunnel can restrict loading of certain cargoes and must be considered when planning the loading of ships.

Ship Measurement

Some of the different types of ships measurements have already been mentioned as bases for charging of ships dues. There are also a number of other statistics or measures needed to be known and understood by agents either for navigational purposes, cargo handling or chartering and sale and purchase purposes.

The following passages will explain the types and purposes of most of the measurements an agent will need to know.

Gross and Nett (Register) Tonnage

One of the earliest attempts used to describe the size or capacity of a ship was to count how many standard barrels or tuns it could carry. This may seem strange until it is remembered that 200 - 300 years ago every manner of goods, dry or liquid, were stored in such barrels. By basing the figure on the number of barrels rather than the weight contained in them it will be noted that this is a volume rather than weight measurement.

Originally ships had only one tonnage entered on the register this being the whole enclosed volume of the ship less the wheelhouse, bakehouse, and toilets constructed above deck. With the advent of the steam engine some governments recognised the advantage of having a modern fleet of mechanically propelled vessels. In order to encourage the installation of engines a reduction in the tonnage was allowed to cover the space taken up by the engine and any crew accomodation, and non-cargo space.

The original tonnage became known as the Gross Registered Tonnage (GRT) and the lower figure as the Nett Registered Tonnage (NRT).

Ships now had a gross and nett registered tonnage. In the mean time the size of a ton had been fixed at an accepted standard of 100 cubic feet.

Different Governments had allowed different reductions for the engine space some allowing up to 30% more for basically similar ships.

To redress this difference the International Tonnage Convention (ITC) of 1969 laid down rules applicable to all vessels worldwide. This convention came into full force in 1994. The size of a ton however has not been standardised for all vessels and now works on a sliding scale. A ton now varies between 95 and 105 cu ft depending on the size and type of vessel. To distinguish the figures arrived at under the new convention the word Registered was dropped and ships now have Gross and Nett tonnages (GT and NT.) Some countries have continued to accept the older measurements and it is important for the agents to ensure that when discussing tonnages the right terminology is used so as to distinguish between the two systems.

Gross and Net Registered tonnages have been the main basis of charging for port dues or determining the application of IMO conventions for so long that shipowners have tried many ingenious ways to reduce their impact.

For charging purposes the open or closed shelter decker was developed. This type of ship had its uppermost deck constructed in such a way that it was not continuous. A special opening known as the 'Tonnage hole' was made in the top deck which could be closed by means of removable hatch coverings. When there were only a small volume of cargo available the hole would be left uncovered, (Open shelter deck) but for larger cargoes the hatch cover would be used giving more covered space available for cargo (Closed shelter deck). Vessels constructed in this manner would be assigned two separate sets of tonnages which would be indicated by means of a triangular 'tonnage mark' carved near the loadline. Ports were quick to catch onto this attempt at avoiding charges and most ports altered their charging systems to recognise only the higher tonnage.

The various IMO conventions and some national legislation impose stricter conditions on larger vessels. Generally the stricter conditions come in at some multiple of 500 Gross or Net tonnages. Shipowners employed naval architects to design vessels with tonnages a ton or so under the nearest point at which more onerous conditions would apply. Ships designed with this in mind are commonly referred to as 'paragraph ships'.

Sizes and weights of respective vessels

Suez and Panama Tonnages

The world's two greatest man-made waterways have each adopted a unique way of measuring ships tonnages. Based on Gross and Net Registered Tons slightly different regulations are made for what must be included or allowed as deductions.

DWT

This is the deadweight in metric tonnes of the ship when carrying a full cargo and stores as permitted by the loadline. It is used as the basis of charging for some port dues and in the UK and Ireland for agency fee purposes.

DWCC

Closely allied to the last , the deadweight cargo capacity of a ship is the weight in metric tonnes of cargo which can be carried when fully loaded as permitted by the loadline. It is used mainly for chartering purposes. The figure usually quoted as the DWCC is that when the ship is carrying a full complement of bunkers and stores. For operational purposes this figure is often exceeded by way of reducing the amount of bunkers etc. carried. This does not jeopardize safety as the full bunker capacity of the ship is rarely needed to complete a voyage with a reasonable margin of bunkers remaining.

LWT

Lightweight is the weight in metric tonnes of the vessel without any cargo, or stores of any kind. Its use is of most interest when a vessel is being sold for demolition since it represents the weight of metal and other materials used in the ships construction.

Grain Cubic or Capacity

Expressed in either cubic metres or cubic feet this is the total volume of cargo space of the vessel. It is used when calculating the amount of cargoes of bulk materials such as grain, sugar, fertilisers etc. which can be loaded on a vessel.

Bale Cubic or Capacity

Like the last this is a volume measurement but in this case the measurement is taken only as far as the inner surfaces of cargo battens or ribs. It is supposed to represent the amount of baled or bagged cargo which can be loaded. The actual quantity of course depends upon how much space is taken up by broken stow and dunnage.

LOA

Length overall - the extreme length of the vessel including any bulbous bow if applicable. This measurement is important for navigational purposes and may also be used for some charges particularly tonnage or berth dues.

Beam

The extreme breadth of the ship. Measured at its widest part. Needs to be known for navigational purposes and also may be important for cargo handling if the reach of equipment is limited.

Depth

Measured from the keel to the underside of the uppermost continuous deck. It is of little significance to an agent except in rare cases where cargo handling equipment can only be used within a certain range above the waterline. Deduction of the vessels draught from the depth will give an indication of the freeboard which can then be determined as in or out side the range of the cargo handling gear.

Draught

Often written as draft this is the distance between the waterline and the keel. Of vital importance for navigational purposes it is also used to calculate some charges particularly pilotage. Great care should be taken when using draughts as a vessels draught will vary along the length of the vessel and also from port to starboard if the vessel is listing.

Air Draught

The distance between the waterline and the highest part of the vessels equipment or superstructure. Of particular importance when vessels need to pass under bridges or other obstructions. A large number of Sea-River vessels have retractable wheelhouses allowing them to pass under bridges. In dealing with such vessels it is important to determine if a quoted airdraught is with the wheelhouse raised or lowered.

Loadline

Not strictly a measurement but of great importance since it establishes the maximum permissible draught for a vessel with a particular cargo at a particular time and in a particular place. Register books generally quote the draught for a vessel loaded to the maximum summer loadline but a vessel may have several different loadlines and it is important to bear this in mind when considering what the draught of a vessel might be or how much cargo can be carried on a voyage. Special marks exist for Fresh water, tropical waters, winter and for timber cargoes. The reasons for different marks being allowed is to take into account the more or less hazardous weather conditions existing in different areas at different times of the year, the different density of water in rivers and canals, and the buoyant effect of timber cargoes.

A vessels loadline marks are always painted amidships on either side of the vessel and will also appear on the vessels loadline certificate. Somewhere above the loadline will be the decl line mark indicating the position of the uppermost continuous deck. The distance between the loadline and the deck mark is the freeboard of the ship. The tonnage mark for vessels assigned dual tonnages will be positioned adjacent to the loadline.

Other Measurements

The deadweight and grain and bale cubics have already been mentioned as of use in determining a vessels carrying capacity. However vessels used for the carriage of containers or Ro Ro cargoes are different means of describing their capacity.

Container vessels are referred to as having a TEU capacity. A TEU or "twenty foot equivalent" this is the space required for the standard 20' 1SO container. Vessels which are able to carry the large 40' containers may be referred to as also having an FEU or "forty foot equivalent unit" capacity.

It should be noted that loading to the maximum TEU capacity of a vessel may not necessarily be permitted as the total weight of containers and cargo therein may exceed the permissible DWCC of the vessel. For this reason when container vessels are offered for sale or charter it is normal to mention the number of TEUS allowed at a range of specified average weights. The capacity of older vessels may not be achievable since containers have increased in height from 8 feet to 8 feet 6 inches, it may not therefore be possible to load the same number of tiers of new containers as of the older variety.

Ro Ro vessels may be used to carry cargo either on standard trailers or in trucks of varying sizes. It is therefore important to know how many of such units may be accommodated. For this reason Ro Ro vessels are described as having a lane metre capacity. This is the total length of lanes of a fixed width available for stowing trucks, trailers etc.

The measurements so far have been concerned with the ship as a whole but for cargo handling purposes it is also necessary to have information about specific parts of the vessel or its equipment.

The number and sizes of individual holds or tanks are important for cargo separation purposes and also to determine if cargo with unusual dimensions can be accommodated in the vessel under deck. Closely allied to hold dimensions are the hatch sizes through which cargo is loaded into the holds.

Older vessels tend to have relatively small hatches and therefore cargo handling can be difficult and slow. The fact that cargo must be moved into the ends and wings of the hold from the space under the hatch opens up the possibility of damage to the cargo. Modern vessels overcome this problem by having hatches which extend over virtually the whole extent of the hold. Hatch covers may be of several types and can be opened either using ships equipment or shore gear. If hatch covers can be removed using shore gear the agent must ensure that cranes of sufficient capacity are available to do this.

The cargo handling gear of the vessel will always have certificates detailing their safe working load. In cases where loading or discharging must be performed using ships gear the certificates must be current and the gear properly maintained. It must be remembered that the quoted capacity of a crane or derrick is the maximum that can be lifted but will reduce the longer the distance the gear is expected to reach.

Further complications can occur on Ro Ro vessels when the trailers and tractor units have incompatible couplings. This can usually be overcome with a little ingenuity on the part of the stevedore.

Tankers must have hoses connected before they can receive or discharge cargo and it may be necessary to determine the lifting capacity of the hose handling crane of a vessel before berthing. The connections between ships pumps and hoses is made at the ships manifold. Most shore installations have universal couplings but occasionally a vessel with non-standard connections may experience delays whilst necessary equipment is located or manufactured. Of interest to agents will be the pumping capability of both shore and vessels pumps as well as the back pressure which can be maintained in order to reduce the possibility of pollution from leakage.

PORT AGENCY

Chapter Ten

PROTECTION AND ORGANISATION

Protection

Throughout this book we have looked at the duties of the agent have and seen them to be varied and sometimes to involve arranging expensive services and handling of large sums of money. We have investigated areas where problems and difficulties can arise. Some of these problems can be the result of mistakes in processing information and documents. Others are caused by negligent acts of any of a number of parties.

The shipowner is able to insure his ship against damage and total loss and the owners of cargo can do the same for their goods. The shipowner as we have seen is likely to suffer other forms of loss which cannot be insured in the normal way by marine insurers.

These losses include cargo claims and surveys, surveys on ships damage, damage claims and surveys on objects damaged by the ship, medical and death benefits for crew, as well as the legal expenses incurred in pursuing payments. To cover these events shipowners almost always become members of a Protection and Indemnity (P&I) Association or Club. The P&I club is a mutual association set up to assist its members in the sort of cases mentioned.

All members are assessed for their risk potential based on ship or fleet size, management systems, past performance, etc. They are then asked to pay an advance subscription or 'call'. The total of advance calls is estimated to be sufficient to cover the likely claims payable on any members behalf. If there happens to be more claims than expected then all members are asked to pay supplementary calls, proportionate to their original call, to cover the cost of the extra claims.

The majority of P&I clubs have selected representatives in most countries who can be called upon at any time to assist a member in a difficult situation. During the course of his work most agents will at some time encounter the owners P&I club. We have seen how an owner may time charter his vessel to another party who will take on some of the risks involved in the running of the ship. Time charterers are able to take out a restricted version of the owner's P&I cover against those claims that may arise out of his operating of the vessel.

The agent is also able to take out cover against his own risks by way of Professional Indemnity cover or Errors and Omissions Insurance. Such cover allows the agent to recover amounts claimed against him or to be financed for legal expenses should he make a mistake which has dire consequences for some other party. We have seen in previous chapters how for example the late presentation of a notice of readiness can mean the owner paying despatch instead of receiving demurrage, or the agent may fail to obtain an original bill of lading when releasing cargo to a party who is later found to have no right to it.

Cover of this nature is not cheap but the premiums will be calculated taking into account several factors. Factors considered will include the volume of the agents business, the type of his business, background details of major principals as well as the agents own past claims record and sometimes the experience and qualifications of the agents key staff.

There are without doubt a great many agents who do operate without such cover to the detriment of their more prudent

188

competitors. Agents with lower costs can try to attract new business by offering lower fees which financially hard pressed owners are more than willing to accept.

Fortunately the growing international trend towards compliance with ISM code for vessel operators and the International ISO 9000 Quality Assurance Standard means that many owners, charterers and cargo interests are not prepared to work with any contractor or sub-contractor who is unable to satisfy their strict approval procedures. The approval procedures may require evidence of professional indemnity insurance or that the agent is fully covered by a ISO 9000 Quality Assurance certificate.

For all agents with, or without, professional indemnity cover there are many practical steps which can be taken to reduce the risks involved in commercial matters.

First and foremost of these is to understand that although both the owner and the agent know of the relationship between themselves, third parties are not in a position to know, and should not be assumed to know.

Concealing a principals identity from a competitor is one thing, concealing it from a provider of goods or services is quite another. One of the first rules that all agents learn is to order goods and services and to sign documents 'as agents only'. This is a step in the right direction but is in itself insufficient to remove all the risks from the agent, which come into effect by virtue of his signature. Signing 'as agents only' certainly alerts the supplier that there is another party who is likely to be responsible for the charges he will impose, but it does not identify him. The agent will find that in certain circumstances he will be legally liable for the debts of undisclosed principals. Where the parties involved are providing and paying for services on a regular basis the agent may be able to prove that the identity of his principal was indeed known to the supplier. Where there is no history of relationships the agent should take pains to sign 'as agents for.................. only', inserting the name and place of business of his principal. The supplier then has the option to consider and reject the supplying of goods or services on credit if he so wishes.

PORT AGENCY

Agents also may become lax when ordering goods and services using such phrases as 'our ship' or 'we have a ship'. This possessive language can lead an unsuspecting third party to believe that the ship actually belongs to the agent who would therefore be responsible. It is much better to use language that clearly indicates the agents position and the level of responsibility he is prepared to accept.

The agent who has received advance funds to cover the expected costs of the call may feel that he need not be so careful as he has money to cover the owners costs. This may be so but the agent should remember that unexpected additional costs can occur at any time and that advance funds received suddenly become insufficient for the owner's debts.

The agent must be prepared to accept that some suppliers, especially those whose services are lowest in value, may decide not to deal with him if he is personally unable to guarantee the payment of debts. Likely candidates to adopt this attitude include taxi services, notaries, dentists and doctors, garbage disposal firms and shipchandlers. To continue working as agents without being able to provide these elements would soon lead to the agent being discredited and so he has to ensure that he does whatever is necessary to keep them happy, even to the extent of paying them out of his own pocket.

Larger suppliers are more likely to take action against the ship and her owner provided the agent has not concealed their identity.

Having taken steps to allow others to fully appreciate the relationship between himself and his principal, the agent should make certain that both he and his principal understand what each requires and expects from the other.

The agent who is to be appointed as a port agent or a general agent for a shipowner on an indefinite basis would be advised to enter into a freely negotiated written contract covering all the normal duties and as many unusual ones as can be easily identified. Clear and concise terms must be included to cover procedures and the agents role in case of emergencies and unexpected events. When contracts are entered into it is usual for both parties to be co-operative and helpful to each other. It is an unfortunate fact that in many cases this goodwill is short lived and will end in acrimony and the courts. It is for this reason that properly thought out contracts and agreements will contain clauses that detail the limits of each parties liability towards the other and penalties for less severe matters.

For the agent who has to compete for each and every appointment the situation is a little different. All agents should have a set of standard conditions which they are prepared to work under. When any appointment is pursued by the agent he should submit those conditions to the owner. The owner is almost certain to have a set of conditions of his own which he will wish to impose, guaranteed to be different from those ofthe agents. In the negotiations that follow each party will have to concede some points. In some countries agency conditions are imposed by law, but in many others standard conditions are published by the National Ship's Agency Association. Often these will be registered with appropriate official bodies such as 'Fair Trading Offices' or Chambers of Commerce.

Agents standard conditions should not be so one sided as to put off a prospective owner principal. Certainly the agents professionalism has to be recognised by way of a reasonable fee but the owner also has a right to expect the agents to be knowledgeable, conscientious and to act in the owners interests at all times. Both parties must recognise that the result of any wrong or negligent act should not be a burden on the innocent party and both should be prepared to assist the other in all ways possible.

Agents who are appointed by owners under the terms of a charter allowing the agent to be selected by the charterer should be especially aware of their rights and responsibilities. There may be some reservation about the agent by the owner and possibly a degree of disinterest from the agent to the owner. These attitudes are recipes for acrimonious disputes and legal actions as soon as one party makes a mistake or creates a problem for the other.

Organisation

The world of shipping towards the end of the 20th century is vastly different from that of even 30-40 years ago. Modern methods of communication are instantaneous which means that information, problems and solutions can be passing between ships, agents, owners and charterers 24 hours a day 365 days of the year.

The agent of today must be equipped to handle this communications revolution and be able to understand and work with faxes, mobile phones, satellites, e-mail as well as older systems such as cable and telex. The electronic transmission of shipping documents is already with us and the advent of paperless systems may not be too far away. In order to cope the need for computers is evident as is the ability to operate them.

It is imperative that the modern agent has ways of being contacted and contacting others at all hours of the day and night. How this is done is of course down to the proprietors and directors of the agency company. Some opt to man their offices 24 hrs a day, others will have a duty phone which can be switched between different staff members on a rota basis to allow coverage when the office is closed. For some agents all staff members are expected to give their home or mobile numbers as emergency contacts. Faxes, telexes and e-mails can be accessed from almost any home computer equipped with the right software and links to the head office.

The boarding of ships is often left to relatively junior staff who may not have sufficient experience or authority to solve problems as they arise. Attending a ship on a wet winters night is an experience that the senior personnel are more than happy to forego and to pass on to their younger colleagues but they should always ensure that back up is available if needed.

Agency work is very much a hands on job and successful companies must recognise that their staff are their only real asset. Proper training of new personnel must not be neglected if the company is to remain successful and should be considered as an obligation of both the employee and the employer. Local education bodies may run courses in shipping matters but the only internationally recognised qualifications are those of The Institute of Chartered Shipbrokers based in London, U.K.

Many countries have a national ship's agent or brokers association which can provide companies with a forum to discuss matters of common interest as well as promoting the agents views on important matters. Where such associations exist they will probably be members of FONASBA the Federation of National Associations of Ship Brokers and Agents.

PORT AGENCY

PORT AGENCY